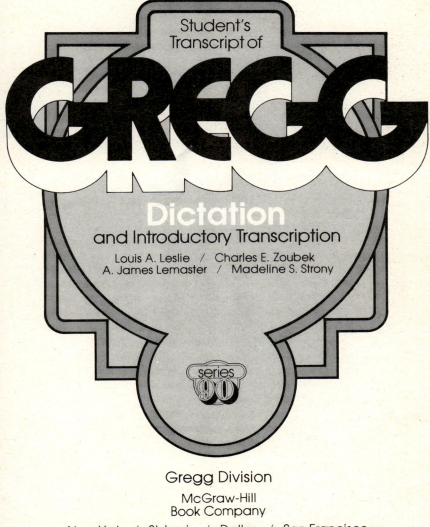

Student's
Transcript of

GREGG

Dictation
and Introductory Transcription

Louis A. Leslie / Charles E. Zoubek
A. James Lemaster / Madeline S. Strony

series
90

Gregg Division

McGraw-Hill
Book Company

New York / St. Louis / Dallas / San Francisco
Auckland / Bogotá / Düsseldorf / Johannesburg / London
Madrid / Mexico / Montreal / New Delhi / Panama / Paris
São Paulo / Singapore / Sydney / Tokyo / Toronto

234567890 **SMSM** 86543210

ISBN 0-07-037736-7

Explanation to Users of This Booklet

This booklet contains the transcript to the shorthand material in the Reading and Writing Practice exercises of *Gregg Dictation and Introductory Transcription, Series 90*. The number preceding each exercise corresponds to the shorthand exercise number in the text, *Gregg Dictation and Introductory Transcription, Series 90*. This transcript will serve two desirable purposes:

1 It will enable the students to look up the word or phrase represented by any outline about which they are in doubt. They will thus be able to cover the Reading and Writing Practice exercises more quickly and with a minimum of discouragement.

2 Because the key is counted in groups of 20 standard words, the teacher will be able to dictate from it.

The Publishers

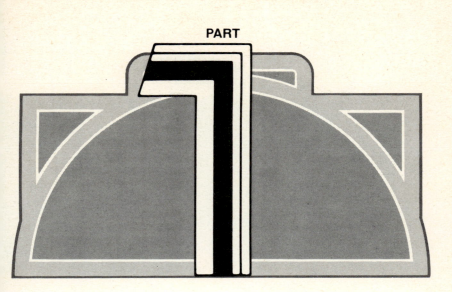

PART

Chapters 1-4
Lessons 1-20

Transcript of Shorthand

(The material is counted in groups of 20 standard words or 28 syllables for convenience in timing the reading or dictation.)

CHAPTER 1

LESSON 1

2 Dear Mrs. Smith: If a very good friend suddenly stopped seeing you without any apparent cause, I am sure[1] you would want to know why.

You suddenly stopped placing your orders with us, and we are wondering why.

It has been[2] nearly six months since you have been in our store. We are, of course, human, and it is quite possible that we have done[3] something that displeased you. Or perhaps we failed to do something you would have liked us to do. If that is the case, please[4] come in and let us do something about it. You will find us ready to listen and to make any adjustment[5] that will once again make you one of our satisfied customers.

This is a particularly good time to come[6] in as our new line of summer clothes arrived a few days ago. Sincerely yours, [134]

4 Dear Mr. Johnson: We sincerely appreciate the complimentary remarks you made about our service[1] in your letter of July 3. I assure you that we will do everything in our power to continue to[2] deserve them.

We are now processing your order of Monday, July 5, and it should be ready for shipment in[3] a few days. You should have the merchandise in plenty of time for your August sale.

We face one problem, however.[4] There is an imminent trucking strike. Let us hope that this labor dispute can be settled quickly. Cordially yours,[5] [100]

5 Dear Mrs. Lopez: Several days ago your friend, Mrs. Leslie C. Green, visited our women's department[1] and purchased a number of dresses. She told our clerk that she came to us on your recommendation. She quoted[2] you as saying that you have been buying your dresses from us for three or four years and that you have always been[3] delighted with the quality of our materials, our prices, and our service.

We are grateful to you, Mrs.[4] Lopez, for sending Mrs. Green to us. We sincerely appreciate it when a customer recommends a[5] friend, for it is an indication that we are providing the type of merchandise and service that our customers[6] want and appreciate. Sincerely yours, [128]

6 Dear Lee: I am attaching a copy of a letter I received from A. J. White, president of the National[1] Picture Company, in which he writes me of the fine service you rendered him in planning his latest advertising[2] campaign.

I appreciate the work you did on this account, and I am confident that your efforts will[3] result in substantial business from the National Picture Company.

The next time you are in the office, Lee,[4] be sure to stop in to see me. I want a complete, detailed report on how you won Mr. White over. Cordially[5] yours,   [101]

7   Dear Janet: I was both happy and sad to hear of your appointment as general sales manager of Benson[1] and Company. I was happy to see you obtain the promotion that you richly deserve, but I was sad because[2] you will no longer be calling on us. We will miss your cheerful, helpful monthly visits.

I am sure you know[3] that you have the best wishes of all of us here. Stop in to see us if your duties as general sales manager[4] ever bring you back to Newark. Sincerely yours, [90]

8   Dear Ed: Thank you for your Christmas card and the friendly, thoughtful message you wrote on it. It was a genuine pleasure[1] to hear from you after so many years and to learn that you are enjoying your retirement.

It has been[2] ten years since you retired, and in that time countless changes have taken place. I am afraid that you would not find[3] many familiar faces if you were to visit us today.

I will probably be in Miami early[4] in September, and at that time I will call you. Perhaps we can get together for a few hours and talk about[5] the good old times.

I hope that your Christmas was a merry one and that Santa Claus was good to you. Sincerely yours,[6] [120]

9   Dear Mr. Anderson: After many months of planning and decorating, we will open the doors of our new[1] store in Troy to the public on January 15.

On January 14 we will have a special preview[2] for our old friends beginning at 5 p.m. At 6 p.m. we will have a buffet dinner.

I hope that you[3] will be able to attend this preview. Will you please be good enough to let us know on the enclosed card whether[4] we may expect you. Sincerely yours,   [87]

10   Dear Mr. Jones: Haven't you at one time or another been faced with the problem that is now confronting us? A[1] customer of ours has stopped sending us orders, and we are wondering why. He was a very good customer,[2] and we cannot afford to lose his business.

At one time you used to order from us regularly. During the[3] last few months, however, we have heard nothing from you. Are you unhappy with our goods, our services, or our prices?[4]

Won't you tell us why we seem to have lost your friendship, Mr. Jones. Please be frank. Do not be afraid of treading[5] on someone's toes. Sincerely yours,   [106]

LESSON 2

15   Mrs. Short: I was glad to learn that you were elected executive vice president of the World Advertising[1] Association on Friday, June 18. This is a timely, well-deserved recognition of the worthwhile[2] contribution you have made to the advertising industry in general and to our organization[3] in particular.

Please feel free to take whatever time is necessary from your work to run the affairs of[4] that organization. In addition, Mrs. Short, don't hesitate to request the help of your associates[5] when they can be of assistance to you.

Please accept my congratulations on your election. We are all proud[6] of you. A. B. Gates [124]

16 Dear Mr. Worth: I have just learned from our sales manager, Mrs. Lynn Davis, that she has convinced you to accept[1] a position as our representative in the states of Tennessee, Kentucky, and Illinois. May I, as[2] president, extend to you a warm welcome to our organization.

I am confident, Mr. Worth, that you[3] will find our organization a friendly one that offers its people every opportunity to succeed[4] and to build for themselves lucrative, satisfying careers.

Please stop in to see me while you are in Chicago[5] for your basic training if you have an opportunity. It will be a pleasure to welcome you personally[6] to our family of employees. Sincerely yours, [130]

17 Dear Jim: I cannot tell you how much Barbara and I enjoyed the party you arranged in honor of my[1] twenty-fifth anniversary with the Hartford Manufacturing Company. I was touched by the many kind things[2] you and my other associates said about me and my contribution to the organization. I assure[3] you, Jim, that it was a lucky day for me when I entered the employ of the Hartford Manufacturing[4] Company as a young salesman in New Jersey and Connecticut.

Thanks for the television set that you[5] presented to me on behalf of the company. I will think of every member of the staff each time I watch a[6] program. Thanks, too, for the scroll signed by all the members of the staff. It will find a place of honor in my den.

Please[7] express my appreciation to everyone who had a part in the planning of the party. Sincerely yours,[8] [160]

18 Dear Ms. Garcia: Mr. James Gray, our present representative in the states of California, Oregon,[1] and Washington, has decided to leave us and accept a position with a New Jersey manufacturer.[2] I have had the good fortune to be designated to take over his territory except southern[3] California.

I realize, of course, that it will not be easy to fill Mr. Gray's shoes, but I assure you[4] I will make every effort to give you the same helpful, personal service that won him so many friends.

I will[5] be in San Francisco on Thursday, February 1, at which time I hope to have the opportunity to meet[6] you and to show you samples of our line of summer merchandise. Sincerely yours, [134]

19 Dear Jane: May I take advantage of this opportunity to congratulate you on the very successful[1] conclusion of your first year as our representative in California, Oregon, and Washington. I[2] have just studied the final sales figures for the year, and I find that you have increased the business in all your large[3] cities except Los Angeles. I am particularly impressed with the success you have had throughout the San[4] Francisco area.

I am confident, Jane, that your sales performance during the coming year will be even[5] more impressive.

Keep up the good work. J. C. Green [109]

20 Dear Mr. Torres: Our representative, Ms. Mary Wilson, will call on you shortly. I hope, Mr. Torres,[1] that you will not feel she is trying to high-pressure you into placing an order.

Her main job, of course, is to[2] sell our products, but her first obligation is to study your special requirements and make sound, practical[3] recommendations. We have found that this policy works to the advantage of all concerned.

Please don't hesitate to[4] take Ms. Wilson into your confidence. She is a specialist in the area of office machines, and I[5] know she will be only too glad to work with you if you will give her the opportunity. Sincerely yours, [119]

LESSON 3

24 Dear Ms. Anderson: It is my pleasure to inform you that your friend and neighbor, Mrs. Janice Temple, has ordered[1] a bushel of Florida oranges as a Christmas gift for you.

These oranges will be available[2] for shipment between January 15 and March 1. Please fill out, sign, and mail the enclosed form when you are ready[3] to receive the oranges.

We are sure, Ms. Anderson, that you and your family will enjoy the delicious[4] flavor of these oranges.

We wish you a very merry Christmas. Sincerely yours, [96]

25 Dear Mrs. Taylor: Thank you for opening a savings account at the Madison Savings Bank. I assure you[1] that it gives me, as president, great pleasure to welcome you as a depositor.

I am enclosing a booklet[2] that describes all the services that are available to you, Mrs. Taylor. We hope that you will take[3] advantage of these services as often as you need them.

It is not necessary for you to come into the[4] bank whenever you wish to make deposits or withdrawals. You can use our drive-in window. This window is open[5] from 9 a.m. until 4 p.m. every weekday except Saturday. On Saturday it is open from[6] 9 a.m. until 12 noon.

There is a free parking lot located behind the bank, and you are welcome to use[7] it if you find it more convenient to transact your business inside the bank. Sincerely yours, [157]

26 Dear Mr. Moore: Would you like to receive our informative and interesting eight-page pamphlet, *Making Mailing*[1] *Lists Pay?* This pamphlet will show you how to obtain the greatest possible income from your investment in your mailing[2] lists. It will be a pleasure, Mr. Moore, to send you one with our compliments upon receipt of the enclosed[3] form.

The information in this leaflet is the result of our many years of practical, successful mail-order[4] experience. It explains the things you can do to increase your efficiency by making better use of[5] your mailing lists.

Send for your copy today. Sincerely yours, [111]

27 Dear Mr. Thomas: We appreciate your letter of Tuesday, April 18, expressing interest in our[1] stationery products. Our leaflet, *Paper Processing*, is enclosed. We believe you will enjoy reading the fascinating[2] information that it contains about paper.

We are also enclosing a copy of our latest[3] price list.

I hope, Mr. Thomas, that we will have the pleasure of adding you to our long list of stationery[4] dealers. Sincerely yours, [84]

28 Dear Mrs. Parks: I deeply appreciate your thoughtfulness in taking the time to talk to our sales staff at our[1] annual sales meeting in Los Angeles. All the representatives had many nice things to say about your[2] presentation.

The information you gave us about the new advertising booklets which you designed to promote[3] our products will be of great help to all of us. Thank you sincerely for your excellent cooperation.[4] I hope that we may call on you again next year to make a similar presentation. Cordially yours, [98]

29 Dear Mr. Simmons: Welcome to Mountain View. I am sure you are going to like our section of Wisconsin. The[1] population of Mountain View has more than doubled in the past five years, but it has retained the charm of a small[2] village.

May I invite you and your family to be our guests for dinner at the Mountain View Inn after you[3] are settled in your new home. People from all over Wisconsin come to this colorful old inn to enjoy its[4] interesting atmosphere and its excellent food.

Mountain View Inn is located at the corner of Maple[5] and Vine Streets.

Call us when you would like to come, and we will reserve a table for you. Once you have tasted the[6] specialties of our experienced chefs, Mr. Simmons, we are confident that you will dine at Mountain View Inn[7] frequently. Sincerely yours, [144]

30 Dear Fred: The bearer of this letter, Harry S. Parker, is a friend of my son. Harry is helping in a survey[1] conducted by our local business bureau to determine how it can serve small businesses more efficiently.[2] He would like a few minutes of your time, Fred, to ask you some questions about your business.

I know you will enjoy[3] meeting Harry. He is intelligent, eager, and personable. I will be deeply grateful for any[4] courtesies you may show him.

Please let me know the next time you are in San Francisco. It would be a pleasure to[5] have you as my guest for luncheon or dinner. Sincerely yours, [111]

LESSON 4

34 Dear Mr. Martin: It will be a pleasure to meet your representative, Miss Carla Brown, and to give her an[1] opportunity to tell us about your new pension plan. We are always interested in learning about[2] new, forward-looking developments in the pension area, and Miss Brown will receive a warm welcome. We will[3] be glad to see her on Wednesday, May 15, at 2 o'clock in our conference room on the first floor of our building.⁴

It is only fair to tell you, however, that we are well satisfied with the company that is presently⁵ managing our pension plan, and the possibility of our changing companies at this time is unlikely.⁶ Yours very truly, [124]

35 Dear Mr. White: We have just read in the Saturday, August 21, *Cleveland Register* that you have been¹ appointed vice president in charge of sales for the Swenson Manufacturing Company and that you will soon move² to the home office in Chicago. We offer you our hearty congratulations.

We are sure that you, your wife,³ and your children do not relish the thought of packing and wrapping and then unpacking and unwrapping your possessions⁴ when you move. You do not have to subject yourself and your family to this chore. Simply call American⁵ Vans, and we will make your moving day a painless one.

A complete description of our services is given in⁶ the enclosed booklet. Take a few minutes now to read it, Mr. White. Then call us at 555-1187⁷ and arrange for our representative to visit you and give you an estimate of the cost of moving.⁸ Sincerely yours, [163]

36 Dear Ms. Harris: I have just received from the printer a copy of your book, *Our World Today*. I think it is one¹ of the most attractive, beautifully illustrated books we have ever produced.

I realize, of course, that² you spent many years writing your book, but I hope you will look back on those years of effort with much satisfaction³ as you leaf through the pages of the book.

I am confident, Ms. Harris, that *Our World Today* will exceed our fondest⁴ expectations in terms of sales.

We look forward to the opportunity of publishing your next book.⁵ Sincerely yours, [102]

37 Dear Mr. Jackson: Many thanks for the part you played in making my trip to Los Angeles one that I will not¹ soon forget. I appreciate the time you took from the responsibilities of your job to show me the sights² of the city and to introduce me to some of your friends.

I am sure that your business will bring you to Newark³ in the near future. My feelings will be deeply wounded, Mr. Jackson, if you don't let me know when that time comes⁴ so that I can reciprocate for your many kindnesses. Sincerely yours, [94]

38 Dear Dr. Clark: I recently attended the fifteenth annual conference of the New York Chemical¹ Society. At one of the meetings I had the pleasure of hearing your director of research, Dr. Kenneth² Lee, speak on the subject of new developments in chemistry. It was an experience that neither I nor³ the 30 other attendees will soon forget.

He spoke for almost an hour, and during that time he had all of⁴ us sitting on the edge of our seats. He presented his ideas well and at the same time kept us entertained⁵ with his delightful sense of humor.

May I express to you, as president of your organization, our[6] appreciation for making it possible for Dr. Lee to be with us. Yours very truly, [137]

39   Dear Jane: I ran into Bill Smith at a meeting of retailers at the Hotel Baker, and he told me that you[1] have just moved into a corner office with drapes and wall-to-wall carpeting and that on the door of the office[2] is a sign that says "Vice President in Charge of Sales."

It is wonderful news. Your promotion is a just recognition[3] of the contribution you have made to the National Manufacturing Company during the past[4] 20 years.

The next time I am in Los Angeles I am going to stop in to see that office and to[5] congratulate its new occupant! Sincerely yours,   [109]

40   Dear Fred: Thank you very much for your letter of congratulations. On January 15 I did receive[1] a promotion here at the National Manufacturing Company. I am, of course, very happy to have[2] this new position.

I am afraid, though, that Bill Smith was a little too lavish in his description of my office.[3] It is a corner office, but you won't find any wall-to-wall carpeting!

Seriously, Fred, do stop in[4] to see me the next time you are in Los Angeles. I will tell you about some of the plans I have made for the[5] future of the company. Your suggestions, of course, will always be welcome. Please let me know if there is anything[6] we can do for your company in the meantime. Sincerely yours,   [132]

41   Dear Charles: Thanks for your thoughtful letter of Monday, January 11, congratulating me on my[1] appointment as sales manager of James and Company. I have been on the job only two weeks, and already I[2] have run into several perplexing problems that are not going to be easy to solve.

I will arrive in[3] Seattle on Sunday evening, February 14, for a sales conference to be held on February 15,[4] 16, and 17. I will call you when I arrive. Perhaps we could have dinner together so that we[5] can discuss my problems. Sincerely yours, [107]

LESSON 5

44   Dear Lloyd: Yesterday I read the announcement in the financial section of the *Daily Times* that your company[1] has purchased the beautiful new ten-story building on East Main Street in Seattle and that you will move into[2] your new quarters on Monday, January 15.

This certainly speaks well of the progress you have made during[3] the past 15 years. I well remember the three-room suite you rented on West Street when you started your business with[4] two assistants and a secretary.

Sometime in February I plan to pay you a visit in your new building,[5] and I hope to have a grand tour of your facilities. Sincerely yours,
[114]

45   Dear Arlene: It was thoughtful of you to write me about our move to the new ten-story building on East Main Street.[1] The new building will give us the room we so sorely need and provide us with additional space for expansion[2] as well. We are all quite excited about the move.

I remember vividly, of course, my first office and my[3] staff of three people. Those were anxious days. I was not sure our company would survive during the first year or two,[4] but it did. Our organization was able to grow rapidly with the help of many competent people.[5] I remember, too, the encouragement and advice you gave me during those early days.

I will be expecting[6] a visit from you shortly after we move in and are settled. You will indeed get the grand tour! Sincerely yours,[7]   [140]

46 Dear Roy: My secretary forwarded to me here in Spain a copy of the Friday, April 16, edition[1] of the *Westport Tribune* containing the announcement of your promotion to the vice presidency of the[2] United Toy Company. She knew that I would be delighted to learn about it.

I have long felt that you have[3] played an indispensable part in the growth that the United Toy Company has enjoyed during the past decade.[4] Your promotion, Roy, is simply a well-deserved recognition of your contribution.

I will be back from[5] Spain on May 15, and at that time I want to congratulate you personally. I will call you so that we[6] can have lunch together. Sincerely yours,   [127]

47 Dear Ms. Brown: August 25 may be just another day to you, but it is a very important one for[1] us. It marks the first anniversary of your opening a checking account at the Union Trust Company.[2] We hope

8 Lesson 5

that you have been well satisfied with the services we have rendered you.

May I express to you the[3] gratitude of the officers of the Union Trust Company for entrusting your banking business to us, Ms. Brown.[4] We hope that you will always feel free to consult us on any financial matters in which our counsel may be[5] helpful. Cordially yours,   [104]

48 *Business Behavior*
Let us think of business behavior as meaning how you act in the presence of, or toward, others with whom you[1] work. A great deal is included in that brief definition. It covers what you do and how you do it, what you[2] say and how you say it.

The habit of doing and saying the right thing in the right tone and manner begins long[3] before you start working. Surveys show that your habits of conduct in school are usually carried over to a[4] job. If you are on time for class, you will probably be on time for work. If you get along well with your classmates,[5] you will probably get along with your co-workers. There are people, however, who feel that they can be late for[6] class; that they can be absent whenever they please; that they can turn in untidy work; that they can be inconsiderate[7] of others; and that *overnight* they are going to change because on the job they will be paid to do what[8] should be done.

But it does not work that way!

Any list of desirable traits—whether for business or personal[9] application—will be very much like any other. This is true because the qualities needed for personal[10] and social success are the same as those needed for business success. Here are only three of the major traits a[11] secretary needs to be an effective person both in and out of the office.

Consideration for Others.[12] Consideration for others is high on the list of desirable traits. It simply means showing respect for[13] the rights and feelings of those with whom we come in contact.

Tact. Tact in business is usually defined as "the[14] ability to do the right thing at the right time." The secretary who uses a pleasant response to soothe the[15] ruffled feelings of an irate customer is using tact. The person who avoids choosing sides when a bit of[16] office gossip is relayed is using tact (to say nothing of discretion). The secretary's job requires[17] tact every day.

Attitude. While many of us sometimes inwardly resist the alarm clock that signals the start[18] of the business day, most of us really prefer to keep busy. We get satisfaction from doing a good job.[19]

Of course, there may be things about your job you will not like. You may be asked to break a personal appointment at[20] the last moment because of the pressure of work; you may not get the exact vacation you want; a number of[21] unimportant, but annoying, things may occur.

You must, however, weigh the good points against the bad; and, in the[22] long run, you will find the merits usually far outweigh the petty annoyances. It is up to you to make[23] the best of the job you have.

Employers want to give you every opportunity to do well. They are eager[24] to help you, but they are also watching your business behavior.

[492]

CHAPTER 2

LESSON 6

50 Dear Mr. Green: Even though it is only April, we are already beginning to get applications from[1] students who want summer jobs. In the past we have hired three or four students to help in some of our clerical[2] jobs while many of the members of the staff were on vacation. As you know, this year there are no funds in the budget[3] for temporary summer help.

When you receive applications in the future from students who want summer[4] work, please explain our situation to them. Do not send the applications to the personnel department. Yours[5] very truly,   [103]

52 Dear Ms. Walker: As I promised you, I am writing you about your application for a position in our[1] sales department. I wish I could give you good news, but I am afraid I cannot.

Because our sales for the past[2] several months have been disappointing, we have decided as an economy measure not to add to our sales[3] force at this time.

If conditions improve in the future and we are in a position to add sales personnel,[4] we will be glad to get in touch with you.

Thank you, Ms. Walker, for taking the time to come in for an interview[5] and for submitting your credentials to us. Sincerely yours, [111]

53 Dear Miss West: Your application for summer employment has been referred to me. We are glad to know that you think[1] highly enough of our organization to want to work for us. We wish we could act favorably on your[2] application, but we will not need temporary help this year.

We hope that you will be able to find a summer[3] position with some other organization that can take advantage of your knowledge, skill, and talent. Very[4] truly yours,   [83]

54   Dear Mr. Hall: Thank you for taking time from your luncheon hour on Friday, June 12, to tell me about the employment[1] opportunities in your organization. I appreciate your offer to set up a number of[2] interviews with some of your colleagues who might be interested in adding me to their staff.

As you requested,[3] I have prepared a complete, detailed data sheet. You will find four copies enclosed.

I will be available, Mr.[4] Hall, at any time that will be convenient to the interviewers. Sincerely yours,
[97]

55   Dear Mr. Robinson: Now that your formal schooling is almost over, you are probably about to take a[1] very important step from the classroom to the business office. That is why we invite you to talk to a member[2] of our personnel department before you decide on that first step.

When you talk to one of our people, you[3] will discover that there are many positions in our organization for which you may be qualified. There[4] are, for example, openings for beginners as stenographers, typists, and business-machine operators.[5]

Why not come in and see for yourself what our organization has to

offer. To arrange an appointment, please[6] call the number given at the top of this letter. Sincerely yours,
[133]

56   Dear Mrs. Allen: When I returned to the office this morning, I found a memorandum on my desk announcing[1] your resignation from our organization and your acceptance of a management position with Rogers[2] and Company in Tennessee.

As I am sure you are aware, I am disappointed that you are leaving[3] us, but I am satisfied that this change in positions is only another step in your rise to prominence[4] in the investment business.

You leave us, Mrs. Allen, with our best wishes and our appreciation of the[5] contribution you have made to the growth and development of our company. If you are in our area[6] in the future, please drop in for a visit. Sincerely yours,   [131]

LESSON 7

61   Dear Ms. King: Regardless of the state of the economy, employees ordinarily continue to take[1] their vacations and are sometimes away from work because of illness or some other legitimate reason. This[2] can have a great effect on your business. We know, for we have been providing temporary personnel to business[3] firms in Philadelphia during good times and bad for more than 30 years.

We have helped publishers,[4] manufacturers, and various other business executives to save money, and we can probably do the same[5] for you.

Try us the next time you need

temporary help. When you call us, we will send you immediately any[6] number of temporary employees who have been carefully screened, tested, and matched to your particular[7] needs.

We are awaiting your call. Cordially yours, [149]

62 Dear Dr. Young: The woman whose picture appears on the enclosed circular is Miss Helen Baker, a customer[1] service representative for Minnesota Temporary Help at one of our branches in St. Paul. She[2] is highly trained in testing skills and in assigning part-time personnel.

Miss Baker visits her customers[3] regularly to discuss their temporary help needs. When one of her people is on the job, she follows up to[4] make sure that the customer is getting all the office skills that are expected.

The next time you would like that kind[5] of service, Dr. Young, call us. We will send Miss Baker to see you and discuss your needs with you. Sincerely yours,[6] [120]

63 Dear Mrs. Nelson: As every business executive will agree, it is usually very difficult to[1] predict how much help a business will need at any given time. Orders may have been heavy yesterday, and they[2] may have been light today. No one ever really knows what they will be tomorrow.

But if you use Miami[3] Temporary-Help Service, this won't affect you. We will send you the help you need to get each day's job done easily[4] and efficiently. When the job is done, our people leave. You pay only for the time each person actually[5] works.

Let us tell you how Miami Temporary-Help Service can enable you to increase your productivity[6] and cut costs.

Call us at 555-1166. Cordially yours, [134]

64 To the Staff: On July 10 Dr. Roger Baker will take over the newly created position of[1] supervisor of urban projects in the states of Pennsylvania, Ohio, and Indiana. He will[2] operate out of our Indianapolis office.

Because of the extraordinary and difficult problems[3] that are affecting big cities throughout the nation at this time, we consider it necessary to place[4] greater emphasis on our efforts in those cities. Dr. Baker's ten years' experience with the State Housing[5] Department in Boston, Massachusetts, will be of great value to him in discharging the responsibilities[6] of his new position.

I know that you all join me in wishing Dr. Baker every success in his new,[7] challenging undertaking. Mary Green [147]

65 Dear Mr. Wright: We regret that you have decided for personal reasons not to come with us when we move our[1] plant from Des Moines, Iowa, to Minneapolis, Minnesota, next spring. We wish it had been possible for[2] you to make this move because, in our opinion, you are a very valuable employee. The loss of your[3] services will have a serious effect on the efficiency of your department.

We had planned to expand[4] your department in the coming year to include two new employees, which would have enabled us to increase our[5] volume of business. It will, of course, be much more difficult to do this without your services.

I hope that you[6] quickly find a position in which your fine talents can be utilized to utmost advantage. Needless to say,[7] you can call on us if you need a reference or recommendation. Yours very truly, [157]

66 Dear Dr. Baker: It is with sincere regret that I am submitting my resignation as a member[1] of your staff.

On Monday, August 30, I was offered a position with the General Manufacturing[2] Company in Florida at a salary considerably higher than the one I am presently receiving.[3]

It has been a pleasure working with you and the other members of your department. My main consideration[4] now, Dr. Baker, is to help you in every way I can in training my successor, for I want my leaving[5] to cause as little inconvenience as possible.

If it will be satisfactory to you, I will[6] be glad to stay until October 15. Sincerely yours, [131]

LESSON 8

70 Dear Mr. Hill: I have been informed by the president of the company that you have decided to accept[1] an appointment to the staff of the public relations department. It gives me great pleasure, Mr. Hill, to extend[2] to you a warm welcome to our family of employees.

In our organization there are many[3] opportunities for our employees to rise to higher positions of responsibility. We follow the[4] policy

of promoting from inside the organization, and only on rare occasions do we go outside[5] for managerial talent.

I am confident that you will be happy with us, and I wish you a bright,[6] profitable future with our organization. Cordially yours, [133]

71 Dear Mrs. Scott: Six weeks have passed since you were kind enough to grant me an interview for the stenographic[1] opening that you had available in the advertising department of your business office in[2] Indianapolis, Indiana. At that time you told me you were interviewing several other students but that[3] you would notify me of your decision by Tuesday, January 15.

I am very much interested[4] in working for the Bell Manufacturing Company. But as I have not yet received a reply, I am[5] inquiring whether someone has already been appointed to the position.

Won't you take a moment to write[6] me your decision. Very truly yours, [127]

72 Dear Mr. Adams: I am happy to be able to recommend Tom White to you without reservation. Tom[1] has been a friend of the family for many years, and it is a pleasure to put in a good word for him.

I[2] wish to give you assurance, however, that friendship is not the sole basis of my recommendation. I know[3] Mr. William Smith, Tom's last employer, and he has great confidence in Tom's ability. He has nothing but[4] praise for the contribution Tom has made to his insurance organization. When Tom decided to leave his[5] former position because of his mother's illness, Mr. Smith was quite disappointed.

I am certain that you[6] will be more than satisfied with Tom's performance. He is a capable, loyal person. He is a man of[7] impeccable integrity who will carry out well any responsibilities you assign to him. Cordially[8] yours,   [161]

73 Mr. Davis: As your records will indicate, I was hired about two years ago as a clerk in the[1] accounting department. During the past two years I have been attending night school at Harper Business College. My studies[2] have included typewriting, shorthand, and business correspondence.

At the present time I can write shorthand at[3] 120 words per minute and can transcribe rapidly and accurately. I wonder, therefore, whether[4] I might be considered for a position in which I could use my stenographic skills. I would, of course, be glad[5] to take the regular dictation and transcription tests that the personnel department gives.

May I have an[6] appointment to discuss this matter at your convenience? E. H. Gates   [133]

74 Miss Green: It gives me great pleasure to welcome you as a new employee in the accounting department of the[1] Ironside Manufacturing Company. I am confident, Miss Green, that you will find our organization[2] a good place to work and that you will find a feeling of friendliness everywhere.

Of course, you must realize that[3] the first few weeks may seem difficult for you, but remember that every beginner has adjustments to make.[4] Remember, too, that everyone on the staff wants you to succeed. If at any time you need help, please don't hesitate[5] to request it from your colleagues.

The best of luck to you in your new position. A. C. Barnes, President
[118]

LESSON 9

78 Dear Mr. Lee: We are looking for dissatisfied people. We are looking for people who are earning between[1] $10,000 and $15,000 a year but who are not getting the self-satisfaction and rewards[2] from their work that their abilities warrant. These are the people we can help. The Interboro Employment[3] Agency specializes in helping people move ahead into jobs that are interesting, appealing, and[4] financially rewarding.

If you are unhappy in your work, the field that you are in does not matter. It could[5] be marketing, finance, or engineering. It is your capabilities that count, and Interboro can help[6] you locate just the job you want.

If you are tired of working in an unrewarding atmosphere, come in for[7] a personal interview. We will discuss your situation with you and guide you into a position that[8] will be both challenging and rewarding. Yours very truly,   [171]

79 Dear Miss Roberts: A technical representative of the Johnson Electric Company is an important[1] link between our company and our clients. This is a person who is self-reliant and who has an understanding[2] of people as well as a thorough knowledge of intricate electronic equipment.

If you would like[3] to be one of our representatives and you meet our qualifications, you will receive intensive basic[4] training at full pay before you are assigned to a locality of your own.

What qualifications must you[5] have? You must have a high school education or its equivalent. You must, of course, have an understanding of[6] the intricate problems of electronics. You must have a pleasant personality. And you must be self-reliant,[7] self-confident, and dependable.

Are you interested? If you are, fill out the enclosed application[8] form and return it to us. If we feel that you are the type of person who has an excellent future as[9] one of our representatives, we will arrange a personal interview with you. Cordially yours, [198]

80 Dear Mr. Mitchell: If you have mechanical aptitude and the ability to meet and work with people,[1] you could become a customer engineer at the National Electronics Company. If you meet our[2] qualifications, you will be assigned to our training division in Westport and will be trained as a customer[3] engineer.

After the completion of your training, you would service and maintain electronic computers,[4] electric copiers, and the other types of electrical equipment that we manufacture.

If you should[5] become a member of our organization, you would enjoy such benefits as a liberal vacation, free[6] life insurance, and refunds for any costs involved for work-related college courses you take.

If you are[7] interested, indicate on the enclosed card a time that would be convenient for you to come in for an interview[8] and forward the card to us. Sincerely yours, [169]

81 Dear Mrs. Campbell: Please accept my sincere thanks for introducing Miss Mary J. Nelson to us. She came in[1] on Wednesday, February 13, for an employment interview, and we were very much impressed with her abilities.[2] She was chosen from among six young men and women who were interviewed on that day for an executive[3] secretarial position.

A surprisingly large number of our employees owe their jobs to people[4] like you who take a friendly, personal interest in our organization.

When you have anyone else to[5] recommend for a position with us, we hope you will let us know. Sincerely yours, [114]

82 Dear Ms. Phillips: Thank you sincerely for the many courtesies you extended to me during our interview[1] on Thursday, March 10. After meeting and talking with the members of your staff to whom you introduced me, I am[2] more convinced than ever that the International Printing Company is the organization with which I[3] would like to make a career.

As I told you, I can start immediately if I am chosen for the opening[4] you have available. My phone number is 555-1188, and I can be reached there at any[5] time after 5 p.m.

It was a privilege, Ms. Phillips, to meet you. Sincerely yours, [116]

LESSON 10

85 To Whom It May Concern: The bearer of this letter is Mr. J. C. Mild, a former employee of ours. Mr.[1] Mild was an account executive in our organization for five years, and during that time he compiled[2] an excellent record.

Because of a sharp decrease in our advertising billings, we have found it necessary[3] to reduce our staff drastically. We have had to let five of our people go, and Mr. Mild was one of them.[4]

If you have an opening for an account executive, we can recommend Mr. Mild to you without[5] reservation. He is a brilliant, hardworking young man with a great deal of creative ability.

If you[6] would like further information about him, I will be more than happy to supply it. Sincerely yours,   [138]

86 Dear Mr. Lopez: We appreciate your interest in our organization as evidenced by your[1] application for a sales position in our international department. Unfortunately, our international[2] business has been rather slow recently, and it has been necessary for us to retrench rather than[3] expand in that area.

It occurs to us, however, that with your fine record in the field of international[4] commerce, you might find a place in such organizations as the General Manufacturing Company,[5] the World Electronics Company, or the National Construction Company.

We hope that you will be[6] successful in finding a position in which you can use your special talents. Sincerely yours,   [137]

87 Dear Miss Carter: A young man by the name of Harry Flint called at our offices on Friday, September 2, and[1] said that you suggested he apply to us for a position.

Mr. Flint told us that he worked for you[2] temporarily, and he seemed eager to have us write to you for his record. We have not written you for his record,[3] however, because we do not have an opening in which we can use his special talents.

Nevertheless, Miss[4] Carter, it speaks well for the good feeling between your organization and ours that you have tried to assist us[5] from an employment standpoint. We appreciate your thoughtfulness. Very truly yours,   [115]

88 To the Staff: On April 12, Mary Howard will assume the post of editor of the new data processing[1] publication division that was authorized by the management board at its last meeting. It will be her[2] responsibility to create a program of data processing materials to be sold in the college[3] market.

Ms. Howard majored in the field of mathematics at Wilson College. She has had considerable[4] experience in systems design and computer programming. In addition, she has taken part in many[5] seminars on data processing.

Ms. Howard will report to J. C. Green, Vice President for Editorial[6] Development, on whose recommendation this appointment is made. L. B. Jennings   [136]

89 Mrs. Evans: As you know, Ms. Fay Billings was appointed correspondence supervisor on December 16[1] last year. She came to us from the National Supplies Company in Boston.

In the six months that she has been[2] with us, she has done a fine job. When she took over, our filing department was in bad shape. She completely[3] reorganized our filing system, and it is now operating efficiently.

Ms. Billings was hired at a[4] salary of $9,000 a year. In view of the contribution she has made to our organization,[5] I recommend that we raise her salary to $11,000. A. B. Stein   [117]

90 To the Staff: On Wednesday, November 10, Miss Martha J. Green was appointed vice president in charge of Washington[1] affairs.

This promotion reflects the growing value of our Washington public affairs office. This office[2] was established three years ago when we recognized the growing impact that government activities were having[3] on our company's operations. It has provided valuable assistance to the company as a[4] whole and to individual departments as well.

In her new position, Miss Green will continue to report[5] to Mr. James Smith, Vice President for Public Affairs. A. B. Jones   [113]

91 *It Pays to Organize*
Mr. Baker, an advertising manager, was one of the few executives in his company to have[1] two secretaries—Betty Crane and Sam Mills. They had finished school at the same time and came highly recommended.[2] When they were tested in the personnel department, Sam scored somewhat higher in taking dictation and in[3] transcribing, but

both scored much better than average.

In the month that Betty and Sam had been on the job, however,[4] Mr. Baker noticed that Betty consistently turned out a good deal more work each day than Sam, even though Sam,[5] according to the application tests, was the more skillful stenographer.

After observing both for a few[6] days, Mr. Baker found the answer. Betty organized her work; Sam did not. Before Betty sat down to transcribe,[7] she made sure she had everything she would need. She checked her stationery and supplies to make certain she had enough;[8] she assembled all the enclosures that were to go into the letters; and she made sure that the reference[9] books she would need were within easy reach. Once she sat down, Betty was able to transcribe with little or no[10] interruption. Sam, on the other hand, was jumping up every few minutes to find something he needed.

Betty proofread[11] her letters while they were still in the typewriter. Sam did not proofread his letters until he had removed them[12] from the machine. When he found an error, he had to reinsert the paper and align it properly before[13] making the correction.

When Mr. Baker pointed out the importance of organizing materials before[14] starting to transcribe, Sam was grateful. It was not long before he was accomplishing far more than before.[15]

Organizing your work will save you time and energy. "Everything you need when and where you need it" is a good motto[16] for the efficient secretary.   [327]

CHAPTER 3

LESSON 11

93 To the Staff: In a few days the local newspapers will carry an announcement of some of our plans for the[1] construction of a new building on Fifth Avenue in the financial district of New York. Construction will begin[2] in a few months, and we hope to be able to move in at the end of next year.

We started planning this building[3] several years ago when it became obvious that our business was going to grow rapidly. I want to[4] thank all of you for your contribution to the growth of the company which has made construction of the new building[5] possible.

I will, of course, inform you from time to time of the progress of the construction and of some of the[6] special features that the building will contain. L. C. Wilson   [131]

96 Dear Mr. Turner: During the past three years our business has grown so rapidly that it has been necessary[1] for us to increase our staff considerably. Our present building, which was erected in 1970[2] when we had only 40 employees, is no longer adequate to meet our space requirements.

We are, therefore,[3] moving to a new, much larger building in January. We will be located at 415 West Street, which[4] is just across the street from the Hotel Baker. We will have four floors in this building, which will take care of our present[5] needs and permit us to expand in the future.

If you are in town on Saturday,

February 20, stop[6] in to visit our new quarters. We will be having a formal open house at that time. Cordially yours,   [138]

97 Mr. Collins: Thank you for the suggestion you placed in the suggestion box a few days ago. A study of[1] your plan, Mr. Collins, convinces us that you have given it a good deal of thought.

We are sorry, however,[2] that we have not been able to adopt it. If we were to make the change you suggest in the lunchroom, it would entail[3] the employment of two or three additional people. The lunchroom, which has been in the red for the past four[4] years, will lose money again this year. Therefore, we do not feel that we would be justified in hiring additional[5] lunchroom employees. Henry L. Benson   [108]

98 Ms. Parker: I have been requested to plan a conference of our managers at which we will discuss the products[1] we will manufacture during the coming year. Tentatively, we will meet on September 18, 19,[2] and 20 at the Hotel Smith in Westport, where we will be away from all office interruptions.

Please let me[3] know which of your products you would like to discuss and how you feel that management can help you.

As time is of the[4] essence, I would appreciate having your suggestions by Monday, August 5, at the latest. R. C. Underwood[5]   [101]

99 To the Sales Staff: On Friday, June 15, at 9 o'clock in the conference room of our main building we will unveil[1] our new Model 16 camera. The features of the camera will be explained by the engineers who[2] developed the camera. We think that this model will revolutionize the entire field of photography.[3]

Please plan to attend this meeting. If you will need a hotel reservation for the night of June 14, return[4] the enclosed card. A. R. Johnson
[87]

100   To the Staff: Now that the old year is on its way out, I would like *to* express to you the appreciation of[1] management for your contribution to what promises to be the most profitable year in our history.[2] It will be some weeks before we have any final figures, but I predict that sales will be more than 20 percent[3] ahead of last year. It is a great record when you consider the depressed condition of our industry[4] in general.

We eagerly look forward to the year ahead, which we expect to be even more profitable[5] *than* this year.

I hope that you and your families will enjoy a delightful Christmas and that the new year will[6] have nothing but good in store for you. C. C. Wilson   [130]

LESSON 12

105   To the Staff: As I wrote you last month, next Tuesday morning, April 13, the southern sales office of the World[1] Manufacturing Company will move from our main building on State Street in Dallas, Texas, to East Worth Street in[2] Atlanta, Georgia.

When members of the other departments of our organization in the main building wish[3] to call the new sales office, they may do so by dialing direct.

There will be a special delivery service[4] for interoffice correspondence and parcels. A messenger will make three trips every day and will pick up any[5] items which have been delivered to the mailing department. There will be no pickups at any other points in[6] this building. If you have any particular questions about this move, I suggest that you call Ms. Underwood[7] at 555-1118. A. R. Parker   [149]

106   Mr. Murphy: Our personnel records show that you have just completed our in-service training course in business[1] organization and management. I hope, Mr. Murphy, that you enjoyed the course and profited from it.

I[2] hope you will be good enough to give us your candid, unbiased opinion of the course. You can do so by filling[3] out the enclosed questionnaire and returning it to our Phoenix, Arizona, office by Wednesday, May 16.[4] Please be frank in your answers.

If you have any particular suggestions on how the course can be improved,[5] we would certainly like to have them. I assure you that your comments will be of great value to us and that they[6] will be kept strictly confidential. A. B. Best   [129]

107   Mr. Cohen: Eight months ago I was hired as a representative of Wilson and Company. My[1] territory consists of the states of Colorado, Utah, and Idaho. While I feel I have made some progress[2] during that time, I am not happy with my territory. I am often away from my home 10, 11,[3] or 12 days per month. In addition, my wife is unhappy in this general area. Therefore, I would like[4] to request a transfer.

I understand that Lee Smith, who has had the states of Texas, New Mexico, and Arizona[5] for the past two years, will no longer be working in Texas. I would be grateful if you would transfer me[6] to that state. M. H. Overman   [126]

108 Mr. Overman: I have discussed your request for a transfer with Mary Jones, our sales manager, and both she[1] and I feel that granting your request at this time would not be in your best interest or that of the company.[2]

It has always been our policy to keep an agent in a particular territory for a period[3] of at least two years. If we were to transfer a representative before that time, we could lose the advantage[4] of the contacts that have been made. In addition, we would have to invest immediately in the training[5] of a replacement.

You, too, would lose the benefit of the time you have invested in developing new[6] customers and would have to start all over again in a new territory. This, of course, would affect your commissions.[7]

I am sure, Mr. Overman, that you will see the wisdom of this decision and will continue the[8] excellent work you have done during the eight months you have spent in your territory. Judith Parker   [177]

109 Ms. Edwards: Yesterday I studied the financial report for the months of October, November, and December[1] on our operations in Fort Worth and Denver. I was ex-

ceedingly distressed by the decrease in our gross[2] sales in those months as compared with the same months a year ago. According to the report, our sales are down nearly[3] 20 percent.

If we do not increase our sales in the coming months, we will not be able to meet our two-year[4] sales goal of $25 million.

Please schedule a meeting of all department executives to discuss[5] this matter. I suggest that we hold the meeting on January 31. If this date is not convenient[6] for anyone, February 1, 2, or 3 will also be satisfactory for me. Harry C. Baker[7] [140]

110 To the Staff: In keeping with the Christmas spirit, the Employees Club of our organization will once again[1] collect and distribute food, clothing, and gifts to those residents of our city who are poor or disadvantaged.[2] The response to this project *has* always been gratifying in the past. Last year, for example, we collected[3] over 900 items of various kinds.

Please join us this year in our efforts to bring some cheer into the[4] lives of these residents. Anyone wishing *to* donate items is requested to bring them to the cafeteria[5] between December 11 and December 16 and deposit them in one of the receptacles[6] that will be placed there. The room will be open during regular working hours.

If you have any questions about[7] this project, please call me. Doris J. Barnes   [148]

LESSON 13

114 Mr. Best: Once again it is time

for a payroll review for our 5,000 employees.

Attached is a list[1] of the 25 employees under your supervision. The list shows each employee's present salary, the[2] date of the last salary increase, and his or her salary range.

Please fill out Form 5850 giving your[3] recommendations for salary increases and the dates on which they should be effective. If you do not plan[4] to give an increase to an employee, explain the reason fully on page 4 of the form.

Please return the list[5] to me by Thursday, July 6. Harry Wilson [109]

115 To Our Dealers: In the past we have tried to stagger the vacation dates of each of the employees in our two[1] offices. This policy, however, proved to be a disadvantage for some employees who could not take their[2] vacations at the time they wanted them.

This year we are going to try a new, improved plan which has been recommended[3] by the employees. We will close our office at 3116 Main Street from July 1 through July[4] 21. Our office at 2501 Jackson Avenue will be closed August 1 through August 21. We[5] will maintain only a skeleton force at each location during these vacation periods.

Won't you help us[6] make this plan succeed by placing now all orders that you would normally place in July and August. Even though[7] your orders will be shipped somewhat earlier than in the past, you will be billed for them at the regular time in[8] September.

Thank you for your cooperation. Very truly yours, [173]

116 To the Staff: Although we have always been proud of our pension plan, we have continually examined it to[1] see whether it could be further improved. Three times since 1970 we have made significant changes in[2] the plan. I am happy to announce that once again, with the approval of the board, we are making two extremely[3] important improvements in the plan to take effect on January 1.

The first improvement reduces[4] the amount paid by most participants and increases the amount paid by the company. The other improvement[5] increases the size of the pension at retirement. We estimate that these revisions will cost the company[6] more than $2 million a year.

The details of these changes are given in the attached folder. As you[7] read the folder, you will realize how the changes affect your own pension.

If you have any questions after[8] you have read the folder, please call the personnel department by dialing 555-1261. William[9] C. Harrington [183]

117 Dear Mr. Peterson: The National Arts Club will hold its annual luncheon meeting on Sunday, February[1] 18, at the Benton Hotel at 1418 Fifth Avenue, Denver, Colorado 80202.[2] Twenty new members will be inducted into the club at that time.

I would appreciate it if you would let me[3] know promptly whether you plan to attend. A self-addressed, stamped card is enclosed for your convenience. Sincerely[4] yours, [81]

118 Ms. Cook: I have just received from Ms. Mary J. Green, one of the typists in my department, an application[1] for a leave of absence for two months. Mary's mother, who lives in Chicago, is ill, and Mary has assumed the[2] task *of* nursing her back to health.

Mary is a competent employee, and I would not want to lose her. I[3] recommend, therefore, that we grant Mary's request *for* a leave of absence.

Her application is attached. James Burns [79]

LESSON 14

122 To the Staff: Many of us at Johnson and Company have in the past received Christmas gifts from our suppliers.[1] Everyone likes to receive Christmas gifts; we are no exception.

However, the acceptance of Christmas gifts by[2] our employees has led to some problems. We have decided on a policy, therefore, that no employee should[3] accept any gifts this year. To implement this policy, we will write to all suppliers, but first we want to[4] be sure that we have your cooperation.

If you receive a gift from a supplier, please turn it over to[5] your manager. Your manager will then see that the gift is returned with a letter explaining our policy.[6] Thus you will not be personally embarrassed.

Thank you for your cooperation. Allen Schultz [137]

123 To the Staff: Federal and state laws prohibit public corporations like ours from making political[1] contributions. As you are undoubtedly aware from reading the newspapers, violations of these provisions[2] frequently result in criminal liability.

We have always complied with these laws, and we have no knowledge[3] of any past violations. However, we believe it desirable at this time to emphasize our[4] long-standing policy of barring the use of corporate funds in any political election.

This[5] policy applies only to the use of company funds. It does not interfere with the rights of employees to[6] use their own personal funds to support any political candidates of their own choice. E. B. Casey [139]

124 To the Staff: Social security taxes are going up again this year; consequently, it is more important[1] than ever that you make sure your earnings are being correctly credited to your account.

A simple way[2] to check the government's record of your earnings is to send in a special card that is available from the[3] personnel department. We encourage you to do so.

Like everyone else, the government can make a mistake.[4] When it improperly records your social security earnings, the mistake must be corrected in three years[5] or a correction may not be possible. Along with your statement of earnings, the government will send you a[6] booklet that tells you how to proceed if you find an error. Dan Wilson [133]

125 To the Members of the Management Committee: We have been most fortunate to be able to persuade Dr.[1] Carl C. Samuels, who is a professor of economics at Wilson College, to talk to our committee[2] about the present condition of our economy. He will endeavor to relate his talk to the problems³ of our own industry.

I believe that all members of the committee will find his presentation extremely⁴ enlightening, enjoyable, and stimulating. At the close of his talk, Dr. Samuels will be glad to⁵ discuss any questions that you may have.

The meeting will be held on Friday, April 12, in Room 2155 at⁶ 11 o'clock in the morning; luncheon will be served at 12 noon.

I hope that you can attend this meeting. Please⁷ let my secretary, R. L. Green, know whether or not we may expect you. A. B. Schwartz [157]

126 Dear Ms. Rogers: We want to welcome you as a new employee of the International Import and Export¹ Company. I am confident that you will find our organization a friendly, interesting place *to* work.² We are a large company, but we are not so large that we cannot take a personal interest in the welfare³ of each employee.

I am enclosing a booklet that tells you all about the people *who* run our⁴ organization, the products that we manufacture, and the services that we render. Please read the booklet; it will⁵ take you only a few minutes.

Your opportunities with us are limited only by your own efforts and⁶ your own ambition. Good luck on your new job, Ms. Rogers. Sincerely yours, [133]

LESSON 15

129 Mr. Starr: When I attended

the spring meeting of the Executives Club last week, I learned of an interesting¹ program that the Miami Manufacturing Company recently instituted. It is called the "Dial² Management" program. Employees of the company can pick up an internal telephone and ask a question³ of management. The query is recorded, transcribed, and passed along to the president, the vice president,⁴ or another company representative who answers the query in writing, usually within a day⁵ or two. This program has brought many questions about company policy, working conditions, and promotions;⁶ it has also brought many helpful, worthwhile suggestions.

I recommend that we consider giving this idea⁷ a trial in our organization. Please look into this matter and let me know what would be involved. Charles⁸ H. Day [161]

130 Mrs. Morgan: One of the members of my staff, Mr. James C. King, has applied for a transfer from the credit¹ department to the newly created appliance division. He feels that he has progressed as far as he can² in the credit department and that the new appliance division will offer him a greater challenge. I think³ he is right, and I recommend that we approve Mr. King's application for a transfer.

If this recommendation⁴ meets with your approval, I suggest that his transfer be effective January 5. William J. Butler⁵ [101]

131 To the Staff: Those of you who were in the vicinity of our building last Saturday may have been startled by¹ the sight of fire-fighting equipment in front of our building and of firemen going in and out.

We had[2] no fire in the building; it was a trial run staged by our area fire company in order to[3] familiarize itself with the physical layout of our building and to see what the firemen would have to[4] contend with in an actual fire. The local fire company's response time, based on this trial, was less[5] than five minutes.

Be assured that we have one of the best-constructed, safest buildings in the city. We have taken[6] every precaution to ensure that our employees will have the maximum protection in the event of[7] an actual fire. Lee Green   [146]

132   Dear Ms. Long: For the past month, which has been extremely hot and humid, we have been having considerable[1] difficulty with the air-conditioning system on our floor. Fifteen people in the north end of the floor are freezing;[2] ten people in the south end are sweltering. The system obviously needs adjustment.

I have called William[3] White, the building superintendent, several times to take care of the matter. Each time he assured me that he[4] would; each time he has not fulfilled his promise.

Won't you please use your influence to get some action. If something isn't[5] done soon, I will have a rebellious staff on my hands! Sincerely yours,   [112]

133   Mr. Reed: As you will recall, at our last meeting we agreed that you would study our needs for new products and[1] have a report ready by February 20.

Unfortunately, complications have arisen in our plant[2] in London that will require my presence there during the entire month of February. Under the circumstances,[3] will it be possible for you to complete the report by January 25 so that I can study[4] it and pass it along to the management committee before I leave? I realize that this is placing[5] a burden on you, and I assure you that I would not ask you to move up the date if I could avoid it.

Can[6] you do it? Betty Strong [124]

134   To the Staff: I plan to take my vacation from September 24 to October 15. I have asked Mary[1] Kent to cover for me during that time in case you may have any special needs or new projects to discuss while[2] I am away.

In case there is some matter that Mary cannot resolve, please get in touch with my secretary,[3] Miss Parson. I will leave my itinerary with her, and she will know where to reach me on any given day.[4] Milton Hudson   [83]

135   *The Value of a Good Secretary*
It was Bill's first day on the job as a junior executive, and he was having lunch with his new business friends.[1] "Have you hired a secretary yet, Bill?" he was asked. "I will be interviewing two people this afternoon,"[2] came the reply, "but I am not very excited about it. With all the advances in technology today,[3] I'm sure that there won't even be such a thing as a secretary within a few more years."

Bill's friends smiled at[4] each other and began discussing the value of a good secretary. Here are some of the comments that they[5] made.

"I need a person assisting me who is familiar with my work. I would never be able to keep[6] everything organized by myself."

"My secretary is so good in transcription that he is able to correct[7] the grammatical mistakes that I sometimes make."

"The thing I like best about my secretary is that she[8] can receive criticism without taking it personally. She knows that we both sometimes make mistakes and that[9] we must help each other."

"Reliability is the most important thing to me. My secretary is always[10] there when I need her. She is absent only when she cannot prevent it."

"A good personality is one[11] of the most valuable traits a secretary can possess. My secretary works very hard but never tries[12] to impress people with her efforts. Even when the work is difficult, she is pleasant and optimistic. Her[13] attitude makes the work easier for everyone around her."

"My secretary knows how to handle callers.[14] She knows when to admit visitors and when to make my appointments."

"My secretary is so familiar with[15] our work routine that she can spot errors I have overlooked. My reputation for accuracy is due in[16] large part to her efficiency."

That conversation took place in 1937. For over 40 years[17] Bill has been a business executive, and in that time he has heard many people predict that both secretaries[18] and their shorthand skills would be replaced by other technology. These, however, were people who did not really[19] appreciate the true value of a good secretary. As Bill quickly

learned, there is no substitute for[20] a secretary who can organize, plan, control, and advise. That is why the number of secretaries[21] continues to grow daily. [424]

CHAPTER 4

LESSON 16

137 Dear Mr. Bell: As you know, for the last two or three years we have been sending you each month a copy of our house[1] organ, *The Writer's Guide.* We hope you have enjoyed the issues you have received, Mr. Bell.

We want to continue[2] sending you *The Writer's Guide,* but first we want to know whether your name and address are correctly entered on our[3] mailing list.

Your name and address appear on the enclosed card. If they are correct, simply check the first box. If you[4] have to make any changes, please indicate them in the spaces provided at the bottom of the card.

May we[5] have the completed card as soon as possible. Thank you for your cooperation. Very truly yours, [118]

140 Dear Ms. Kelly: Thank you for your letter and bill dated November 16. I have forwarded to our accounting[1] department your bill for our advertising in the October issue of your magazine, and you should receive[2] payment in a few days.

As you will see from the enclosed marked copy of our advertisement, there are several[3] errors that were not corrected at the proof stage. To prevent similar errors in the future, won't you please[4] have the printer send us proofs before each issue goes to press.

We are now preparing copy for the January[5] issue of the magazine, and you should have it shortly. Sincerely yours, [114]

141 Dear Mr. Wood: At its last meeting on Monday, December 10, the operations committee approved my[1] advertising budget for the coming year. It was the largest, most detailed budget I had ever submitted, and[2] I had a feeling that it would not be approved without some deletions.

One of the major factors that influenced[3] the committee's favorable decision was the report on the nation's economy for next year which[4] appeared in the November issue of *Business Quarterly*. I quoted several paragraphs from that report[5] to buttress my arguments for extra funds for television and radio advertising for the coming[6] year.

Please accept my congratulations on the publication of a very timely report. You and your[7] editors have done an excellent job, Mr. Wood. Sincerely yours, [152]

142 Dear Miss Jennings: A very popular telephone number is 555-5115. That is the number[1] of the classified advertising department of the *Daily Journal*. People call it for a variety[2] of reasons. Some want to sell a house; others want to buy one. Some want to rent an apartment; others want to sublet[3] one.

When these people contact one of the clerks in our classified advertising department, they are pleased to[4] discover that the clerks don't just take their ad. They actually help compose the copy. They offer suggestions[5] that will enable our advertisers to get the most effective ad for the least money.

The next time you have[6] something to sell or something to buy, why not call us at 555-5115. Your ad will bring quick results.[7] Very truly yours, [144]

143 Mr. Stein: I am attaching copy for the advertisement that we are planning to run in several[1] professional magazines during the months of March, April, and May. As you will notice, we are planning to use four[2] colors in this ad, which we have never done before.

If you wish to make any changes, kindly use a red pencil[3] *to* mark them.

Since time is running short and there is still much work to be done on the ad, may I have your comments[4] *by* January 15. John C. Harris [88]

LESSON 17

148 Dear Mr. Bailey: When a publisher comes out with a new magazine, it is not difficult to convince business[1] executives to advertise their goods in the first issue. But the important test comes in the second, third,[2] and fourth issues.

The first issue of *Business World*, which appeared on June 1, had more than 50 full-page advertisements.[3] We already have signed contracts for 60 pages in July and 65 pages in August. This is[4] a definite, clear-cut indication that progressive business executives expect *Business World* to be around[5] for a long time and that they have recognized the wisdom of continuing their advertising with us.

If[6] you want to get your message across to people who are up to date and who make buying decisions, advertise[7] in *Business World*. Our rate card is enclosed. Yours very truly,

[151]

149 Ladies and Gentlemen: All of us value an encouraging word from others, but most of us are much slower[1] than we should be to give an encouraging word to others when they have earned it.

The purpose of this letter[2] is to give your magazine, *News Weekly*, an encouraging pat on the back for its innovative approach and[3] its ability to create new business.

As you know, we operate a chain of first-class apartment buildings[4] in Maryland and Delaware. Occasionally we have vacancies in these buildings that we naturally[5] want to fill expeditiously. Whenever we use the pages of *News Weekly* to advertise vacancies, we[6] fill the vacancies quickly.

We have already instructed our advertising agency to renew[7] immediately our advertising contract with you for the coming year. Cordially yours, [155]

150 Gentlemen: In the December issue of four widely read national magazines, we will run a full-page ad[1] on the Wilmington Electric Shaver. We know from experience that this advertising will stimulate a[2] great deal of interest in our electric shavers and that you and our other dealers will profit from this interest.[3]

To enable you to derive the maxi-

mum benefit from this advertising, we have prepared a four-color[4] enlargement of the page for display in your store windows.

Would you indicate on the enclosed form how many[5] of these enlargements you would like and return it in the postage-paid envelope that is also enclosed. Why not[6] do it now. Yours very truly, [126]

151 Dear Mrs. Ward: Our advertising manager tells me that we have not received copies of the April, May, and[1] June issues of *The Secretary* in which a one-page ad featuring our calculators was to appear. Will[2] you please send us copies of these issues as soon as possible.

We usually get our copies of the publication[3] on time, but on several occasions during the past year we have failed to receive issues in which *we*[4] had purchased advertising.

As I am sure you realize, it is important for us to receive copies of[5] all publications in which our advertising appears. I would appreciate it, therefore, if you would check your[6] mailing list to be sure that we receive each issue at our Delaware office just as soon as *it* comes off the[7] press. Very truly yours, [144]

LESSON 18

155 Dear Ms. Gordon: Thousands of women read and enjoy *The Magazine for Women*, and advertisers know it. That[1] is why a record number of them advertised in our October issue. In fact, advertisers have made *The*[2] *Magazine for Women* the only women's service magazine with six consecutive years of advertising[3] increases.

Why do women prefer our magazine to any other? The reason is simple—we treat them as[4] individuals and not as statistics. Since more women get actively involved with *The Magazine for Women*,[5] more women purchase our advertisers' products.

Would you like to increase your company's business and profits?[6] Then try a full-page ad in *The Magazine for Women*. Sincerely yours, [133]

156 Dear Mr. Jackson: During the past year *Business World* won 12 major awards for editorial excellence.[1] But words aren't all that make a magazine great. Magazines need attractive graphics as well. *Business World* was[2] awarded three medals in this area by the National Graphic Arts Society.

When a magazine has[3] a staff like ours, is it any wonder that we reach more than 4 million of the country's top executives? Is[4] it any wonder that advertisers make us the undisputed leader in business and industrial[5] advertising pages among general magazines?

To get your message across effectively, advertise in[6] *Business World*. Sincerely yours, [125]

157 Dear Miss Griffin: A top executive of one of our nation's largest airlines tells us that *Business World* is the[1] most "stolen" publication on his airline's planes. What he means is that more people deplane with the airline's copies[2] of *Business World* than with its own in-flight magazine, which they are invited to take.

At the last count, 27[3] airlines were buying subscriptions by the thousands and putting them in their planes each week. They know that *Business World*[4] is ideal in-flight reading for their most frequent customers, traveling business executives.

Wouldn't *Business[5] World* be just the place for you to reach these professional men and women with your advertising message? Send[6] for our rate card today, Miss Griffin. Very truly yours, [130]

158 Dear Dr. Howard: It has been our pleasure for the past several years to send you our company's catalogs,[1] illustrative circulars, leaflets, and other materials describing our professional handbooks and[2] industrial publications. We hope, Dr. Howard, that this material has been useful to you.

This year we[3] are undertaking a revision of our mailing list to be sure that only those people who are genuinely[4] interested in our publications receive our advertising.

If you would like to continue receiving[5] our company's advertising, won't you please fill out and mail the enclosed card; it requires no postage. Your[6] cooperation in helping us keep our list up to date will be sincerely appreciated. Cordially yours,[7] [140]

159 To the Staff: As you know, for some time we have been looking for someone *to* head up the television division[1] of our company's advertising department. I am happy to report that Mr. Charles H. Best, who comes to[2] us from the production department of Westport Manufacturing

Company, has been appointed director[3] of that division.

It will be Mr. Best's responsibility to help us make the greatest use of television[4] in the promotion of our entire line *of* professional handbooks and the other materials[5] that we publish for the industrial market.

We feel that Mr. Best is well qualified for this[6] responsibility, and we wish him every success in his new, challenging job. Robert B. Simmons [137]

LESSON 19

163 Dear Mr. Bennett: Please take a few minutes to do something for us that will help us serve you better: Fill out and[1] return the enclosed questionnaire to us at our offices in Richmond, Virginia.

As you know, we send you[2] each month a copy of our magazine, *Advertising Today*. In this magazine, which we send with our compliments,[3] we carefully summarize for our clients the best articles on advertising that appeared in the[4] previous month's technical periodicals that serve the trade. We hope that this magazine has been helpful to you[5] and that it has brought you some new, interesting ideas.

Naturally, we want to make this magazine as[6] useful to our clients as possible. You can help us do so by answering the questions on the enclosed[7] questionnaire. Won't you take a few minutes now to do this. Yours very truly,

PS. Perhaps there are other executives[8] in your organization who would enjoy receiving copies of *Advertising Today*. We will be[9] glad to send them copies if you will give us

their names and addresses. [193]

164 Gentlemen: Last year we had a very restricted advertising budget available to us; we could afford[1] to advertise our office equipment in only one national periodical. We had six[2] periodicals to choose from, and after careful study, we selected yours, *The American Monthly*.

We made no[3] mistake. The 12 advertisements we ran in *The American Monthly* resulted in $250,000[4] worth of business that could be traced directly to our advertising.

Needless to say, we will continue[5] to place a major portion of our office-equipment advertising in *The American Monthly*.[6] Sincerely yours, [122]

165 Dear Mr. Brooks: Do you realize that you may be losing a large volume of profitable business because[1] you have not set up a mail-order department within your organization? This is one sure way to reach[2] additional customers at a low sales cost.

There are thousands of people who prefer to buy by mail. For many[3] of them it is the most convenient way because they cannot easily reach the retail outlets that carry[4] a special product.

Probably some of your own competitors are at the present moment taking advantage[5] of this method of obtaining new customers. This market is also waiting to buy from you— if you know how[6] to reach it.

Let us show you facts and figures without obligation about this rich market and how you can reach[7] it. It will be a pleasure to send one of our representatives from our Baltimore, Maryland, office to[8] see you. Cordially yours, [164]

166 Dear Ms. Watson: Thank you, Ms. Watson, for the courtesy you showed me in our interview in Charleston, West Virginia,[1] on Tuesday, November 10, and for the opportunity to submit an estimate on the cost of printing[2] the circulars you plan to mail to your list of prospects. Although you ultimately chose someone else to do[3] the job, we appreciate your considering the use of our services.

As I am sure I need not tell you,[4] the National Advertising Company will be glad to work with you on any of your mailing needs in the[5] future. We offer high quality, prompt service, and reasonable rates.

When you again plan a mailing, won't you[6] please give us an opportunity to serve you. Sincerely yours, [132]

167 Dear Mr. Gray: Do you know the best place to look when you are searching *for* an apartment, Mr. Gray? It is the[1] classified advertising section of the *Daily Times*, the leading newspaper in Wilmington, Delaware. Every[2] day it contains a big selection of apartments advertised in many locations and in all rent brackets.[3]

If you cannot find an apartment that meets your exact requirements, place *an* advertisement of your own in[4] our classified section. Many house owners prefer to choose their own tenants, and you may be just the tenant they[5] want.

For more information about the *Daily Times* classified ads for apartments, call 555-1181.[6] Sincerely yours, [124]

LESSON 20

170 Dear Mr. Sullivan: You will be interested to know that we have sold more than 100,000 copies[1] of your book, *Advertising Facts*, since its publication five years ago. When you consider the technical nature[2] of the book, this is an incredible record. Congratulations for having written such a fine book.

We[3] should now start thinking seriously about the second edition of *Advertising Facts*. I am sure that you[4] have thought of many new, innovative ways to make the book even better. I think, too, that you will want to give[5] some consideration to the suggestions we have received from those who have used your book in business, in colleges,[6] and in technical institutes.

Could you arrange to attend a conference at our Westfield, Connecticut,[7] office on Monday, December 5, at ten in the morning? Cordially yours, [154]

171 Dear Mrs. Stone: Because of a misunderstanding by a member of our planning department, your client's ad[1] in the January issue of *Business Facts* was printed as a one-column instead of a two-column ad.[2] Please pardon us for this error; we will take steps to see that it does not recur.

The bill we sent you was for[3] $200, which is the price of a two-column ad. Enclosed is a revised bill for $100, which[4] is the price of a one-column ad.

We hope that we will have the pleasure of running your client's advertising[5] for many years to come. Cordially yours, [107]

172 Dear Mr. Myers: It was a pleasure to send you our advertising quotations and some information about[1] our magazine, *The Secretary*. As you will see from the facts in the enclosed folder, our magazine has[2] grown rapidly during the last five years. We are constantly adding new subscribers, and the number of new[3] organizations that advertise in our pages has also increased.

You will note that the advertising rates in[4] the enclosed folder are based on a circulation of 90,000. At this time, however, our circulation[5] is more than 110,000; consequently, by scheduling your ads with us now, you will reach 20,000[6] additional subscribers at no extra cost.

If there is any other information you would like[7] about *The Secretary*, please let me know. I will be very happy to send it to you. Sincerely yours, [159]

173 Dear Ms. Trenton: I used to think that newspapers had a relatively short life. However, we just received a[1] request from one of our customers on a coupon clipped from an advertisement that ran in the *Business Journal*[2] in February, 1975. The coupon requested one of our representatives to call.

Of course,[3] this delayed reaction is not typical. In most cases our advertisements in your paper result in[4] telephone calls the day they are placed as well as coupon responses during the following few days.

I thought you[5] would be interested to know that our ads in the *Business Journal* continue working for us long after they[6] have been placed. Yours truly, [124]

174 Dear Mr. Sloan: Yesterday I talked with a number of members of our promotion staff about advertising[1] in your new magazine, *Business Executive*. They are very much interested in your plans. However, they[2] must soon submit their magazine advertising budget for the balance of the year; therefore, they would appreciate[3] your getting to them promptly the specifications for the new magazine, your advertising rates, and any[4] other material you can send them.

I am confident that we will be able to take some space in the[5] magazine. Before we can make a definite commitment, however, we must have complete, detailed information[6] about your plans. Very truly yours, [127]

175 *Robert Baker, Timesaver*
Robert Baker's employer, Mr. Price, was a public relations executive. Mr. Price's work required[1] him to travel a great deal, and he was often away from the office for a week or two at a time. Upon[2] his return from a trip, he was always eager to catch up on what had happened while he was away.

Robert[3] put all communications that had come in during Mr. Price's absence into one folder. Consequently,[4] before Mr. Price could decide what needed immediate attention and what could wait, he had to go through[5] everything, separating those communications that were urgent from those that were not. Robert noticed this and wondered[6] how he could organize these materials to save time for Mr. Price. After some study he devised a[7] plan for separating Mr. Price's accumulated communications into four labeled folders:

1.[8] *Urgent.* In this folder Robert placed everything that had to be attended to as soon as possible—letters[9] to be answered immediately, telegrams to be acknowledged, and important calls to be made.

2. *Correspondence*[10] *to Be Answered.* Into this folder he put correspondence and other communications that did not need[11] immediate attention but which he knew Mr. Price would want to take care of within the next two or three days.[12]

3. *Correspondence to Be Read.* Into this folder Robert placed letters, memorandums, and other communications[13] that had already been attended to but were left unfiled so that Mr. Price would be informed of the[14] action taken.

4. *Miscellaneous Reading.* In this folder he put reports, bulletins, magazines, and other[15] printed matter that Mr. Price could read at his leisure.

As a secretary you should be on the lookout[16] for ways of making your employer's work easier and more productive. When you make your employer look efficient,[17] you make yourself look efficient too. The result: more promotions and better pay.   [355]

How Big Should My Shorthand Be?

Each writer must set his own size for his shorthand writing. Whatever size seems right to you is probably the best[1] size for you. One skillful shorthand reporter writes 500 words of shorthand on an ordinary notebook page;[2] another writes only 50 words on a similar page. Neither extreme is recommended. If you naturally[3] find yourself writing very large notes or very small notes, you need not be concerned about the size of your notes.[4]

If you write whatever size of shorthand notes seems to be natural for you, the size will have little or no effect[5] on your speed. If you try constantly to write notes larger or smaller than you would naturally write, you may[6] find that the attempt to change the size of your notes hinders the development of your speed. [132]—*Martin J. Dupraw*

Chapters 5-8
Lessons 21-40

CHAPTER 5

LESSON 21

177 Dear Mr. Price: Thank you very much for your order for some of our stationery items. Thank you also for[1] your check for $12. Your order has been filled and shipped, and you should have it in a few days.

Our records show, Mr.[2] Price, that you purchase from us several times each month and always enclose a check in payment. Because of the[3] frequency of your orders, it occurs to us that you might like to have us open a charge account for you. With[4] a charge account, you can place as many orders as you wish each month and pay for them with one check when you receive[5] an invoice.

If you think a charge account with us would be helpful, let us know. It will be a pleasure to open[6] one for you. Cordially yours,   [125]

180 Gentlemen: On Friday, January 28, I sent you an order for four lamps, and I asked that they be[1] charged to the account that I have had with your company for many years. I actually opened this account on[2] May 25, 1970, the day I moved to Chicago, Illinois.

I was very much surprised when[3] on February 1 I received a letter asking me to fill out a long, complicated two-page credit form.[4] Surely there must be some mistake.

Will you please look into this matter. In the meantime, please ship the lamps that I ordered[5] as soon as possible. I must have them by the 28th of February. Cordially yours,   [117]

181 Dear Miss Brown: Please accept my sincere apologies for sending you the credit form intended for charge-account[1] applicants. Obviously, the form was sent to you from our credit department in error. The lamps you ordered[2] have been sent and charged to your regular account No. 10056.

In the future, Miss Brown, we will be[3] able to take care of your orders more expeditiously if you will include your account number on each order.[4] Unless we have this number, we must go through our alphabetic files, and this slows up the processing of your[5] order. We realize that this will take an extra minute or two of your time, but it will help us to serve you[6] better.

We hope that you get many years of fine service from the lamps that you purchased. Yours truly,   [137]

182 Dear Mr. Russell: I doubt very much that March 10 has any special significance for you. It does for us,[1] however. It was March 10, 1976, that we had the pleasure of opening a charge account for[2] you at Wilson's Department Store.

During the years you have used your account frequently to make purchases from our[3] various departments.

We appreciate very much the orders you placed with us, Mr. Russell, and assure[4] you that we will do our best to merit your business in the future.

We hope that we will have many opportunities[5] to serve you. Sincerely yours,   [107]

183 Dear Ms. Richards: At its meeting on Monday, April 16, our management committee decided to make a[1] number of changes in our credit department so that we can serve our customers more expeditiously. One[2] of the most important things we want to do is to revise the series of collection letters we have been using.[3] Our present series has not been very effective.

On April 28 I was told by Mr. Jack H.[4] Brown, president of the Harper Manufacturing Company, that your organization has many collection[5] letters which bring in remittances and retain goodwill at the same time.

Could you let us have copies of these[6] letters so that we can adapt them to our own special needs? Perhaps at sometime in the future we may be able[7] to reciprocate your kindness. Whenever we can be of help to you, just let us know. A self-addressed[8] envelope, which requires no postage, is enclosed for your convenience. Cordially yours, [175]

184 Dear Mr. Harper: A month ago and again two weeks ago we asked you to pay your bill of $85[1] or at least to tell us the reason why you have not paid us. We have heard nothing from you.

Many times credit[2] bureaus write us concerning the bill-paying habits of our customers. We would be very unhappy, Mr.[3] Harper, to report to a credit bureau that you are slow in paying your debts.

Perhaps there is a reason why[4] you have not paid us. If there is, please tell us what it is. Better still, send us your check for $85.[5] Sincerely yours, [102]

185 Dear Mr. Foster: As you know, Thanksgiving comes on the 28th of November *this* year. This means

that you will[1] have less than a month after Thanksgiving to do all your Christmas shopping.

But don't wait until after Thanksgiving[2] to do your shopping; start right now. If you do not have a charge account with us, this would be an ideal time to[3] open one.

We appreciate all our customers, but we treat our *charge*-account customers like members of our[4] family. We send them advance notices of special events and private sales.

If you do your Christmas shopping[5] with us, your charge account will make your shopping easy, fast, and convenient. When we hear from you, we will send you[6] our Christmas catalog. Sincerely yours, [127]

LESSON 22

190 Dear Mr. Henderson: This is a letter from our credit department, but do not be alarmed. Your account is[1] in good order, and we are not asking for a payment of any kind.

You see, Mr. Henderson, our credit[2] department doesn't write only collection letters; it also writes thank-you letters. This is a thank-you letter,[3] the kind every credit manager ordinarily enjoys writing.

Your account has never been overdue,[4] which is something that we cannot say about some of our accounts. Your company's payments have always been on[5] time, and not once have we had to send you so much as a reminder.

It is a pleasure to do business with the[6] General Manufacturing Company. I wish more organizations would take care of their responsibilities[7] as efficiently as you do. Sincerely yours, [150]

191 Dear Sir or Madam: On Monday, June 1, I am moving to Little Rock, where I have accepted a position[1] as correspondence secretary to Mr. George Green, president of the Arkansas Manufacturing[2] Company.

I would like to open a charge account at the Southern Department Store, which I understand is one of[3] the leading department stores in Little Rock. At the present time I have a charge account at several stores in[4] Milwaukee, Wisconsin, to which I refer you for any credit information you may wish about me. The[5] company names and addresses are included on the attached sheet.

Please send any forms that I must fill out to[6] my parents' address, which is 330 Fifth Avenue in Milwaukee. Sincerely yours,   [136]

192 Dear Mrs. Overmeyer: As you will recall, on June 15 you wrote us a commendatory letter for[1] your employee, James C. Barnes, when we asked you for information about his character, integrity, and[2] bill-paying habits. When we read your fine opinion of Mr. Barnes, we opened a charge account for him immediately.[3] He has charged $600 worth of merchandise to this account in August, September, and October,[4] but he has not acknowledged any of our requests for payment.

The address he gave us was 14 East[5] 81 Street, Providence, Rhode Island 02904. Does he still live at this address? If he does not, can you[6] give us his present address? Unless we hear from Mr. Barnes soon, we will have to turn the account over to a[7] collection agency.

Any help you can give us will be appreciated. Sincerely yours,   [157]

193 Gentlemen: Miss Alice Lexington, who lives at 600 Market Street in Jackson, has given us the name of[1] the Louisiana and Mississippi Manufacturing Company as one of those to whom we should write[2] for references concerning her character and financial status. She states that she worked for your organization[3] for the last five years.

Miss Lexington wishes us to ship her one of our accounting machines on an approval[4] basis. Before we make this shipment, however, we would like to have some information about her bill-paying[5] habits.

Any information you care to give us about Miss Lexington will be sincerely appreciated.[6] A stamped, addressed envelope is enclosed for your convenience in writing us. Very truly yours,   [139]

194 Dear Miss Green: We are pleased to tell you that your National credit card account has been reinstated. Your new credit[1] card is being mailed separately.

This is just a friendly reminder that the account must be kept current to avoid[2] another cancellation. As you know, our terms call for payment upon receipt of the monthly statement.

We hope,[3] Miss Green, that you derive much pleasure from the use of your card. Sincerely yours,   [74]

195 Dear Mr. Farmer: Perhaps you have already placed your check in the mail to take care of your July account, and[1] it has crossed this letter in the mail. If that is the case, please disregard this reminder.

However, if you have[2] not yet sent us your remittance, please do so now. Simply slip your check in the enclosed stamped envelope and drop it[3] in the mail. Yours very truly, [65]

196 Dear Mr. Perry: As you know, your account at the Providence Men's Shop is more than a month overdue. It makes[1] us very unhappy, Mr. Perry, to see your account fall so far in arrears. When you are behind in paying[2] your account, you may become a little hesitant about placing further orders. Consequently, both *of*[3] us lose. We lose the business you would have given us; you lose the profit that the sale of our men's clothes would bring.

Take[4] a few minutes now to check your stock and make up an order on those items that are low. Then send us your order[5] and your check *for* $800 in the envelope that is enclosed. Sincerely yours, [116]

LESSON 23

200 Dear Mr. Butler: As I am sure you realize, we appreciate your business; we would be loath to lose it.[1] At the same time, our margin of profit is so small that we cannot carry an account for more than the 30[2] days called for by your contract.

Your account, which amounts to $250, is considerably[3] overdue. While we would like very much to oblige you by granting you a 30-day extension, we cannot see[4] our way clear to do so.

If you cannot pay the entire amount at this time, perhaps you can send us a check for[5] $100. We would then be willing to wait another week or two for the remaining $150.[6]

We are looking forward to receiving a check from you by return mail.

Very truly yours, [138]

201 Dear Miss Arnold: Thank you very much for your letter asking for information about the amount in your checking[1] account. Today your account shows a balance of 98 cents. As you know, this account has not been used in[2] several months, and the monthly charge of 75 cents has nearly depleted the entire account.

We will,[3] of course, be happy to mail you a check for 98 cents, but we hope you will decide to start using your bank[4] account again on a regular basis. Sincerely yours,

PS. Remember, our ready-credit account is[5] available to all regular depositors. [110]

202 Dear Mr. Gold: You will recall that on Monday, July 20, you wrote us a letter apologizing for[1] not having paid your May bill amounting to $1,200 and promising to pay it in full[2] on or before August 15. Here it is September 1, and we still have not received your check or heard from you.[3]

Don't you think, Mr. Gold, that we have been understanding and considerate? Don't you think, too, that you should send us[4] your check for $1,200 without delay?

Write out your check now and send it to us in the stamped,[5] self-addressed envelope that is enclosed. We know that you will feel better after you have done this. We certainly[6] will! Yours truly, [123]

203 Dear Mr. Small: When our representative, Ms. Jane C. Carter, was in the office yesterday, she left with us[1] your order No. 1161 amounting to $401.25. We were particularly pleased to[2] receive this order because it was the first we have had from you.

Before shipping your order, however, we would[3] like to make a routine credit check so that we can give you an accurate rating.

Would you be good enough, Mr.[4] Small, to let us have the name of your bank, the names of other suppliers who have extended credit to you,[5] and any other references that you care to send us.

After we receive this information, it will be only[6] a matter of a few days' time before you will receive your order.

No doubt you make such routine checks yourself.[7] I am sure, therefore, that we can count on you to cooperate with us. Sincerely yours,
[156]

204 Dear Mr. Jenkins: As you will recall, on January 18 you informed us *that* you would place a check in[1] the mail by February 25 to take care of your overdue account amounting *to* $1,000.[2] We were, of course, delighted to have this information.

Thirty days have passed since you made your promise, but we have[3] not yet received the check. We hope, Mr. Jenkins, that we do not have to turn your account over to a collection[4] agency.

Take care of this obligation today; place your check in the mail now. You will be keeping your[5] valuable credit rating, and we will be keeping a good customer. Sincerely yours, [115]

LESSON 24

208 Dear Mrs. Barnes: Perhaps you have experienced the frustration and mortification of having a store refuse[1] to accept your personal check for something you wanted to buy. This will never happen to you again if[2] you have a National identification card. With this card your check will be accepted by any store that[3] displays a National sign. It will be accepted in drugstores, in supermarkets, and in many other places[4] that would not accept your checks before.

When you make your purchase, simply hand your identification card to[5] the clerk along with your check. The card will be inserted into a computer terminal, and in seconds the[6] clerk will receive verification that your check is good. There will be no long, embarrassing delay.

We invite[7] you to stop in at any one of our branches and arrange for a National identification card.[8] When your account is opened, we will give you a directory that lists all the stores in which your card will be honored.[9] Cordially yours,
[183]

209 Dear Mr. Gates: Many thanks for your recent charge-account application.

Before we can open an account for[1] you, however, we will need certain additional information. Perhaps the best way to supply this information[2] to us would be for you to stop in to see me at your convenience. I am in my office weekdays,[3] except Saturdays, from 9 a.m. to 5 p.m. No appointment is necessary.

If it is not possible[4] for you to come in, perhaps you can call me on the telephone.

I am sure that after I have had an[5]

opportunity to talk with you, we will be able to issue you a credit card without delay. Sincerely[6] yours,

[121]

210 Dear Mr. Reynolds: As you know, on Friday, June 12, you purchased from our furniture department on the installment[1] plan a Wilson sofa costing $300. When we sold it to you, you made a deposit of[2] $50 as a down payment and agreed to take care of the remainder in ten monthly payments.

Your payments[3] were on time during the first three months, Mr. Reynolds, but we received no payments in October, November, and[4] December.

Perhaps there are circumstances that prevent you from making your payments, but you have not told us about[5] them; consequently, we cannot be helpful.

Don't delay; send us your check today. If for any reason you[6] cannot do so, call us at 555-1181 between 10 a.m. and 4:30 p.m. Sincerely[7] yours, [141]

211 Dear Ms. Peters: During the past six weeks we have mailed several routine reminders about your past-due account[1] to you at your business address, 1161 West 23 Street, in Los Angeles, California. To[2] date, however, we have received no response to any of these letters.

It may be that there are personal[3] circumstances that would explain your delay in taking care of your account. If there are, please tell us about them.

We[4] realize that errors on our part can occur. If we have made an error in connection with your account,

please[5] let us know. You can call us any weekday after 9 o'clock at 555-6107. Yours very[6] truly, [121]

212 Dear Miss Chan: I have a theory that a credit manager was the inspiration for the invention of[1] the alarm clock. It rings softly at first. The longer it is neglected, however, *the* more persistent it seems[2] to become. Ultimately, the sleeper must do something about it.

Unlike the alarm clock, I do not want *to*[3] appear to be persistent, but it is time for you to do something about your overdue account amounting[4] to $800.

Won't you take a moment now to write us a check and mail it in the enclosed envelope;[5] it requires no postage. If you cannot pay the entire amount immediately, please call me at[6] 555-4107. I will be happy to discuss the matter with you. Cordially yours, [137]

LESSON 25

215 Dear Miss Graham: Thank you for your application for one of our credit cards. I wish I could write you that your[1] application has been accepted. Unfortunately, I cannot give you that good news.

Persons to whom we issue[2] our credit card must meet certain rigid requirements. From the information you have supplied us, you do not meet[3] those requirements fully; consequently, we are unable to issue a card to you at this time.

If you can[4] furnish us with additional information that you feel will enable us to reconsider your application[5] favorably, please let us know. Yours truly, [110]

216 Dear Mr. Simmons: Thank you for submitting your application to obtain a charge account at Wilson's. I wish[1] I could write you that your application has been accepted and that your name has been added to our list of charge[2] customers. Unfortunately, I cannot do so.

Our routine check with the National Credit Bureau indicates[3] that it would be unwise for you to assume any further credit obligations until you are able[4] to reduce the debts that are presently outstanding. We would be delighted, of course, to take care of your needs on[5] a cash basis.

When your financial position improves, we will be glad to reconsider your application[6] for a charge account. I hope, Mr. Simmons, that you understand our position. Sincerely yours,   [137]

217 Dear Mrs. Coles: We are always delighted to receive a request to open a charge account for a customer.[1] We know what a convenience it is to be able to shop in a store, select what you want, and simply[2] say, "Charge it."

We wish that we could make a charge account available to you, but we believe that for the present[3] it would be better for both of us if you were to continue making purchases on a cash basis.

Enclosed[4] is an announcement of our January white sale which starts at 9 o'clock on Tuesday, January 2. Why[5] not come in and take advantage of the savings offered at this sale. Yours sincerely,   [115]

218 Dear Mr. Hamilton: A friend of ours, a well-known banker, made this statement recently: "When people get into[1] debt, they lose their independence."

I had never thought of the matter in just that way. On reflection, however,[2] I can understand what he means.

We like to think of our customers as independent business people who would[3] fight for their economic freedom as well as their political independence. For that reason, Mr.[4] Hamilton, we do not like to see anyone have a delinquent account.

In looking over our records, however,[5] we find a balance of $200 due on your account No. 1150. The balance was[6] payable on July 1.

Won't you regain your freedom by sending us your check today. Cordially yours,   [138]

219 Dear Mr. Smith: The auditors are here making an examination of our books, and they are paying particular[1] attention to our accounts receivable ledger. They are wondering why some of our accounts have not[2] been paid. As you know, your account has not been paid for several months.

Won't you send us your check today, Mr. Smith.[3] If you could send us a check for $200, the entire amount that is due, it would be very much[4] appreciated. If you cannot, send us at least a partial payment and tell us when you will be able to pay[5] the rest.

A stamped, addressed envelope is enclosed for your convenience. Sincerely yours,   [116]

220 *Shh!*

Secrets are hard to keep. It is human nature for us to want to share an exciting piece of information[1] with a friend—especially if it is information that only a few possess. Keeping information[2] confidential is just as much a part of the secretary's job as taking dictation or typing a report.[3]

The word *secretary* means "keeper of secrets." The secretary who cannot keep secrets cannot be a true[4] assistant to an executive.

A secretary who prepares the payroll knows the salaries of all the[5] employees who work for the company. The secretary many times has advance information about those[6] going to get a promotion or those going to be dismissed. The secretary knows about big events that[7] are coming up in the office.

Nothing can be accomplished and great harm may be done if these secrets are betrayed.[8]

Many a secretary has been embarrassed by the careless release of information. How does the secretary[9] remain truthful when asked about something that is to be kept secret? For many secretaries the key[10] word is *official*. They merely say, "I haven't received any official information about the matter.[11] I am sure Mrs. Jones will release the information when it becomes official."

The secretary is being[12] truthful, for information does not become official until it is announced to everyone by a[13] high-ranking executive.

Ask yourself this question: When a friend tells me something and says, "Now this is just between you[14] and me," can I really keep the secret? Or do I pass it along to someone else, saying, "I'm not supposed to[15] tell you this, but . . ."? If you can

develop the habit of keeping confidences now, you will have gone a long way[16] toward meeting an important requirement of your secretarial job.   [333]

CHAPTER 6

LESSON 26

222 Dear Mrs. Rivers: We are sorry to learn that the jacket you ordered from us three or four weeks ago has not[1] yet reached you. Our records show that the jacket was shipped from Dallas on Tuesday, February 7, and should have reached[2] you at least ten days ago.

Because we want to save you further inconvenience, we are shipping you a[3] duplicate today. If you receive our original shipment sometime in the future, please return it to us. We[4] will, of course, be glad to pay the shipping charge.

We hope that you enjoy wearing your attractive new jacket. Sincerely[5] yours,   [101]

225 Mr. Murray: Here is some encouraging, unexpected good news for the sales department of Johnson and[1] Company. As you know, we estimated that our sales for October would be $300,000. When we[2] arrived at that figure, we thought it was optimistic because conditions in our industry were somewhat depressed.[3]

On Monday, November 5, I received the final figures from the accounting department for October,[4] and I find that our sales for that month are slightly more than $400,000—or approximately[5] 33 percent over our calculations.

This means that we will probably exceed our year-end budget of[6] $6 million.

Congratulations on your staff's wonderful sales performance. A. B. Green [136]

226 Ms. Green: Thank you for the encouraging report of our sales for October. Actually, we did even better[1] than the figures indicate. It seems that an order for $25,000 that we received on October[2] 28 and filled on October 29 was not included in the final figures. One of the record[3] clerks in the accounting department was absent from October 27 through November 1 and did[4] not include the order in the October report. It will, however, appear in the November report.

I[5] think there is no question that we will exceed our year-end budget of $6 million. Edward B. Murray [119]

227 To the Sales Staff: As you know, for some time the General Manufacturing Company has been sending you our[1] monthly bulletin, *Company News,* which gives you information of a personal nature about the people[2] on our sales staff. I have felt, and still feel, that sales representatives are interested in what other people on[3] the staff are doing. They want to know when one of them marries, has a baby, or distinguishes himself or herself[4] in some way.

I will be glad to continue issuing *Company News,* but I must have your help. Some members[5] of the staff have faithfully sent me notes of general interest for the bulletins; some, however, have not.[6]

If you come across some bit of information that you think might be of interest to the other representatives,[7] I hope you will send it to me. Your cooperation will be greatly appreciated. Alan C.[8] Baker [161]

228 Dear Fred: The final sales figures for the National Retail Company have just been released, and I have very[1] good news for you. You are one of the most successful sales representatives in our entire organization.[2]

You increased sales in Memphis, Tennessee, by more than 30 percent over last year, which is a remarkable[3] achievement when you consider that this is only your second year in that area.

Congratulations, Fred,[4] on a great sales job. Joseph L. Gates [87]

229 Dear Mr. McDonald: Because of the current paper shortage, the General Printing Company had to reduce[1] substantially the printing order for our annual catalog. However, we have reserved a catalog[2] for you because you have been a good customer of ours for many years.

This catalog *will* enable you[3] to pick out the things you want and order them by mail, which is one of the most convenient ways to do your shopping.[4] To receive your catalog, simply detach the top half of the enclosed card and mail it *to* our order[5] department; the card requires no postage. Sincerely yours, [110]

LESSON 27

234 Dear Mr. Alexander: Enclosed is a catalog in which we have published more than 300 ideas[1] for unusual presents for regular holidays or special occasions. These things come from all over the world;[2] they are made by some of the world's finest, best-known designers and manufacturers.

Choosing a present is easy,[3] quick, and convenient when you shop from this catalog. You do all your shopping from the comfort of your home.[4]

Select as many things as you wish. Then order them and inspect them in your own home for 15 days to be sure[5] that they are exactly what you wish to have. If after 15 days' time you are not completely satisfied with[6] them, you can send them back to us. That will be the end of the transaction.

If you prefer, you can charge everything[7] you purchase to your National credit account. Cordially yours,   [152]

235 Dear Stockholder: You will be glad to hear that our company achieved record sales in the second quarter of this[1] year.

During the spring of this year, we opened 2 new stores in Oklahoma City, which increases the number[2] in our chain to 40 stores. We have also modernized each of our stores in the states of Kansas, Montana, and[3] Nebraska.

Scheduled for opening this fall are 4 more new stores here in Oklahoma. These new stores will add[4] 360,000 square feet of store area.

Our outlook for the second half of the fiscal year, which[5] ordinarily brings in the major portion of our income, is one of great expectations. Cordially yours,   [119]

236 Dear David: I know that you have been eagerly waiting to hear the results of the sales aptitude tests you took[1] on March 21.

The results of your tests on social attributes and basic business skills are very flattering.[2] They indicate, however, that your talents would not be fully utilized in sales work. We feel, therefore, that[3] we cannot offer you the sales opening we have here in Tulsa, Oklahoma.

I realize, David, that[4] this decision will be a disappointment to you, but it was made with our mutual best interests in mind.

I[5] wish you the best of success in finding a position in which your many talents may be utilized to their[6] full extent. Sincerely yours,
[125]

237 Dear Ms. Clark: I received the good news this morning that you have accepted the position as our representative[1] in the states of North Dakota and South Dakota. I understand that you have given your present[2] organization one month's notice and that you will report to our home office at 1441 South Main Street here in[3] Fargo, North Dakota, on Monday, February 1.

When you arrive here, you will take an intensive three-week sales[4] training course, which I am sure you will find very worthwhile. You will then spend three weeks on the road with our sales manager,[5] Mr. Steven Clay, who is a master sales representative. After that, you will be on your own.

We look[6] forward to welcoming you aboard on February 1. Sincerely yours,   [133]

238 Mr. Day: At its meeting on

Wednesday, April 18, the management committee decided *to* adopt your[1] suggestion to make two sales territories out of the states of Oklahoma and Nebraska. As you requested,[2] you will keep Oklahoma; we will place a new representative in Nebraska as soon as another[3] qualified person can be found.

If you know any people to recommend for the job, please have *them* call me to[4] arrange an interview in Omaha.

Congratulations, Mr. Day, on the fine job you have done in the past.[5] Keep up the good work. A. B. Jones [106]

LESSON 28

242 Dear Mr. Nathan: We have just been notified that our lease will not be renewed and that we must vacate our[1] premises before Sunday, May 1. Because of the difficulty of finding a suitable place to relocate,[2] we are going out of business. As I am sure you realize, our getting out of the clothing business was not[3] an easy decision. We have served the clothing needs of the men of Lincoln over a period of 30[4] years.

As a result of our decision, we are offering our entire stock of men's clothing at prices that are[5] substantially lower than wholesale prices.

We are giving our charge customers an opportunity to make[6] their selections before we announce our closing to the public. On April 2, 3, and 4 our doors will be open[7] only to charge customers; after April 4 the general public will be welcome.

So plan to come in[8] during our special sale days; you will be gratified with the savings you will make.

Sincerely yours, [177]

243 Dear Mr. Jordan: I have just made an embarrassing discovery. Somehow the letters inviting our customers[1] to visit our booth at the Commercial Office Equipment Exhibit in Wichita, Kansas, were mailed with[2] insufficient postage. I cannot explain how this happened, but I am having the matter investigated.[3]

I think it is essential, however, that we take immediate steps to rectify this serious error.[4] I suggest, therefore, that you write a brief, courteous letter of apology to our customers as soon as[5] possible. I will appreciate your taking care of this matter, which is of great concern to me. Charles C. Curtis[6] [121]

244 Dear Mr. Page: You will recall that you gave us a firm delivery date of August 10 on the 26 cassettes[1] we ordered from you on June 20. That date was satisfactory at the time because the sales personnel[2] who are to receive these cassettes were not scheduled to meet until August 20.

This meeting, however, had to[3] be moved up to August 1. Consequently, it is imperative that we have the cassettes by July 25[4] so that they will be available to our sales personnel at the meeting.

If you could meet that new date, we[5] will be extremely grateful. We realize that this request for earlier shipment places a substantial burden[6] on you, and we assure you we would not make it unless the reason for it was compelling. Cordially yours,[7] [140]

245 Dear Mr. Baker: Your request that we move up the delivery date of the 26 cassettes you ordered from[1] August 10 to July 25 poses something of a problem for us. As you know, this is our rush season,[2] and our factory is working to full capacity. However, because you have been such a good customer in[3] the past, we will make a special effort to comply with your request.

We hope that your people will be happy with[4] the cassettes. Sincerely yours, [85]

246 Dear Jim: When I returned to the office from a long business trip, I found on my desk a duplicate report of[1] your visit with Mr. Frank C. Wilson, president of the National Distributing Company. I gather[2] that Mr. Wilson said some unkind things about the quality of our products and our various services[3] and that *you* gave him a piece of your mind.

Perhaps you felt somewhat better when you told him what you thought. How are you[4] going to feel, though, when you call on him on your next trip? You realize, of course, that you will have to call on him[5] because we need his business.

An even more crucial consideration is how *he* is going to feel.

I am[6] going to offer you some friendly advice, Jim. Write him a note saying that you are sorry. Your apologizing[7] will make things a little easier for you the next time you *call* on him. B. B. Green [156]

LESSON 29

250 Dear Mr. Smith: Do you remember the "good old days" last year when things actually cost 5 percent less than they do[1] today? We

do, and we are determined to bring them back. We are turning our clocks back one fiscal year from today[2] until Christmas. During this time we will deduct 5 percent from your bill for everything you purchase. This is a[3] bold attempt on our part to make this Christmas just as merry as last year's.

So plan to do your Christmas shopping at[4] the Western Department Store and save 5 percent on everything you purchase. We look forward to seeing you. Very[5] truly yours, [103]

251 Dear Mr. Snyder: You will find enclosed a copy of the agenda for our annual sales meeting, which will[1] be held in Albany during the week of December 1. As you will see on page 3 of the agenda, your[2] presentation is scheduled for Thursday, December 4, from 10 a.m. to 12 noon.

At this sales meeting there will[3] be about 20 new travelers who are eagerly awaiting your ideas on how they can increase sales[4] in their territories.

Please feel free, Mr. Snyder, to attend any of the other meetings that may be of[5] interest to you.

My secretary, Ms. Helen C. White, is making hotel reservations for you in[6] Albany. When she receives a confirmation, she will forward it to you. If there is any other information[7] you would like about the meeting, please call me. Yours very truly, [153]

252 Dear Mr. Ford: Several days ago we received a telephone inquiry from Miss Mary Paul, a purchasing[1] agent for the Johnson Manufacturing Company, about our wood products. We called on her and made a[2] quotation. Before we departed, we had an order with a promise of more orders to come.

We asked her frankly[3] why she had not called on us before, and her reply prompted us to write this letter to you. She said that she[4] expected the prices of a large, well-known manufacturer like our company to be quite high.

You, too, may[5] have the impression that our prices are high. That is not so. Our modern methods of production make it possible[6] for us to manufacture our products economically and sell them at reasonable prices.

Let us[7] prepare an estimate for you on your requirements the next time you are in the market for wood products. Sincerely[8] yours, [161]

253 Dear Mr. Davis: As you know, paper was in short supply last year. Almost all producers raised their prices to[1] their dealers during this time of shortage. However, we at the National Paper Company held the line on[2] our prices despite our decreasing profits.

This year the situation will be even more depressing. Paper[3] will again be in very short supply. We have no alternative, therefore, but to increase our prices. A new[4] schedule of prices is enclosed; it will go into effect on September 1. Very truly yours, [98]

254 To the Staff: I have just received the good news from the accounting department that our division exceeded its[1] sales and profit budget for last year by almost 8 percent. This is a great performance,

and it was possible[2] only because of your dedicated efforts.

As you may know, our budget for the coming year *is* a big one.[3] It calls for an increase of 12 percent in sales. To meet this budget, we will have to put forth even greater effort[4] *than* last year.

For five consecutive years our division has made its sales and profit budget, and I am[5] confident that we will reach it this year also.

Thank you for an outstanding job in the past; I know you will do an[6] even greater job in the future. William H. Day [130]

LESSON 30

257 Mr. Young: Frank Smith, who has represented us for the past 15 years in the Midwest, resigned on December[1] 1 to open his own insurance agency in Tulsa, Oklahoma. Frank made a definite contribution[2] to our organization during his years on our staff, and we are sorry to lose him. He leaves us with our[3] best wishes for success in his new endeavor.

To replace Frank, we were fortunate to obtain the services[4] of Ann H. Jones. She comes to us from the Johnson Office Equipment Company, which recently closed its plant in[5] Omaha. I am quite sure you will like and respect her.

Ann will be calling on you soon to meet your people and[6] to learn how she can best serve your office equipment needs. I know, Mr. Young, that you will accord Ann the same[7] consideration that you always gave Frank. James Watson [150]

258 Dear Mr. Gibson: You will recall that on Thursday, August 18, you purchased eight shirts in the men's department[1] at Mason's Department Store. The shirts were shipped via air express on August 19, and we billed you for[2] $64 on September 1.

We have just discovered, however, that the sales tax and the cost of shipping,[3] amounting to $4, were not included in your bill. We apologize for the mistake.

Won't you be good enough[4] to write a check for the full amount and mail it to us at your convenience in the stamped, self-addressed[5] envelope that is enclosed.

When you again have need for high-quality suits, topcoats, or any other men's apparel,[6] we hope you will come to Mason's. Very truly yours,   [130]

259 Dear Ms. Burns: I will be in Chicago from November 12 to November 19. If it is convenient[1] for you, I would like to have the privilege during my visit of discussing with you some of the products that[2] we manufacture. It will take only a few minutes.

As you know, the National Office Equipment Company[3] is one of the largest and most respected companies in the office equipment field. We have recently[4] developed a new line of small calculators that we believe will revolutionize the electronic[5] calculator field.

Please let me know on the enclosed card when it will be convenient for me to call. Any time[6] between November 12 and November 19 will be convenient for me. Cordially yours,   [137]

260 Dear Mr. Bryant: We were pleased to receive your letter of January 18 expressing interest in[1] stocking our meat products in the Western Supermarket. A copy of our booklet, *Modern Meat Processing*, is[2] on its way to you; you should have it in two or three days. We are sure you will find the booklet quite interesting[3] and informative.

Our representative in your territory, Mr. Charles H. Smith, will call on you the next[4] time he is in your neighborhood. Please feel free to ask him any questions you may have about our products.

It will[5] be a pleasure, Mr. Bryant, to add you to our large list of dealers. Sincerely yours,   [116]

261 Dear Mrs. Jones: We are enclosing a copy of our latest catalog of hardware supplies. It contains[1] several hundred new items at prices that we are sure will please you.

Our first consideration in putting this[2] catalog together was the convenience of our customers. We have tried to make it as easy to refer[3] to as possible, and we believe we have succeeded.

Would you be good enough, Mrs. Jones, to sign and return[4] the enclosed card acknowledging receipt of this catalog. This will help us keep our files up to date. Sincerely[5] yours,   [101]

262 Dear Mr. James: As you know, we have not had a representative in your area since Frank Green retired[1] in April. Since that time we have been looking for just the person to replace him, and we have found him. His name is[2] Bill Wilson, who comes to you with ten years of sales experience.

Bill will call on you during the week of July[3] 15. When you meet him, I think you will be impressed with his eagerness to be of service. Sincerely yours, [79]

263 *Chronic Complainers Not Welcome*

Are you a chronic complainer?

Do you find fault with just about everything?

If so, you might find yourself in the[1] same position as Lynn French. Lynn didn't like his typewriter, his chair was not comfortable, and the office was[2] either too hot or too cold. What's more, Lynn didn't like most of the people with whom he worked or the way things were done.[3]

Of course, everyone has likes and dislikes and no office is perfect, but most people keep any unpleasant thoughts[4] they might have to themselves. Not Lynn! He grumbled constantly to anyone who would listen. "If things don't improve around[5] here . . ." is the way he would begin his frequent threats to quit.

One day another staff member, growing tired of[6] listening to Lynn's gripes, said, "Really, Lynn, we all have our pet peeves and tasks to do that we don't really care for. But[7] we have to adjust and make the most of the situation. Constant grumbling doesn't help; it only makes things[8] worse."

His friend's advice was excellent, but it didn't help Lynn. He went right on complaining. And it was not long before[9] his constant griping reached the ears of the top executives.

Eventually there was nothing for his supervisor[10] to do but call Lynn into his office. "It has been evident to everyone for some time that you are[11] not happy here, Mr. French," he said. "Your attitude has affected your own work and that of others in the office.[12] I think it is best, therefore, that you find a job with another company where you will be happier."

Lynn[13] was stunned. He had been asked to leave! He had not really intended to quit—he was only calling attention to[14] things that "needed improving." He was not as miserable as he pretended; in fact, he rather liked the job[15] and the people. But it was too late. He had no choice but to find another job.

No one wants a griper. The smart[16] office employee tries to find what is right about the office, not what is wrong. In most cases the "rights" far[17] outnumber the "wrongs." [343]

CHAPTER 7

LESSON 31

265 Dear Mrs. Wells: We can, of course, understand your annoyance at the late delivery of your order for six woolen[1] sweaters. We are constantly striving to prevent such situations from developing, but they sometimes happen[2] in spite of our best efforts. We are especially sorry that this late delivery has distressed you because[3] you have been a good friend and customer for many years.

So far, we have not been able to find out what happened.[4] Two or three days ago we started a tracer on the shipment, but it may be several days before we learn[5] anything definite. While this will be of little comfort to you at this time, we may as a result of this[6] tracer be able to prevent similar situations from developing in the future. We want to be[7] sure, Mrs. Wells, that you are not inconvenienced again.

Thank you for your patience and understanding. Sincerely[8] yours,
[161]

268   Gentlemen: When I was in Chicago on November 5, I purchased a tennis outfit from your tennis shop.[1] A copy of my sales slip is enclosed.

I wanted a garment that would be easy to care for, and the label[2] indicated that the outfit could safely be placed in a washing machine. After the first time I washed it, I found[3] that the garment shrank almost three inches. I have not been able to wear it, of course. I am, therefore, returning[4] it to you for refund of $18, the price I paid for it.

Since your store has an enviable reputation[5] of being one of the best in the Midwest, I look forward to receiving your check promptly. Yours truly,[6]
[120]

269   Dear Mrs. Porter: Like every other well-known organization, we try hard to fill all our customers' orders[1] promptly, efficiently, and exactly. But in spite of our best efforts, the people in our organization[2] occasionally make mistakes. Unfortunately, Mrs. Porter, you have been the victim of one of these mistakes,[3] and I want to apologize for it.

Your lamp was placed in a truck which makes deliveries for us in the southern[4] states. It should, of course, have been placed in the truck which delivers in the eastern states.

We are shipping another[5] lamp to

you today by air; you should have it in a few days. Because we are to blame for this delay, we will take[6] care of the shipping charges, which amount to $17.50. Sincerely yours,
[137]

270   Gentlemen: As you will recall, on December 16 I wrote you reporting a shortage of six rugs in the[1] shipment we received from your East Coast wholesale warehouse in Philadelphia. On December 20 you replied[2] that you wanted to check into the matter carefully in order to obtain all pertinent facts and that we[3] would hear from you again shortly.

Today is January 5, but we have not yet heard from you. Have you been able[4] to trace the missing rugs? If you haven't, what do you plan to do?

It is important that I have an answer[5] without delay, for I have a customer interested in purchasing these rugs. Sincerely yours,   [118]

271   Dear Mr. Owens: We were indeed sorry to learn from your letter of February 20 that the bicycle[1] you ordered as a gift for your son's birthday arrived at your house in southern California in such badly damaged[2] condition that you could not accept it.

The express company gave us a receipt acknowledging that the[3] bicycle was properly crated when we delivered it to them; consequently, the damage must have occurred[4] in transit.

We are sending you today by our own truck another bicycle exactly like the one you ordered.[5] It should reach you on or before March 1. The driver will pick up the damaged bicycle.

We hope that your son[6] derives many years of pleasure from his birthday present. Sincerely yours,

[133]

272 Dear Mrs. Green: Enclosed is our new Christmas catalog of gifts.

Each year it is our pleasure to fill your orders[1] for Christmas gifts that your friends and family can enjoy. Each year we make every effort to bring you new ideas[2] for gifts, but we also are sure to include those which have been favorites of our customers year after year.[3]

Select the gifts you want to give and check them on the order form in the catalog. Then mail the form to us. We[4] will do the rest, Mrs. Green. Yours very truly,   [89]

273 Dear Mr. Wagner: We were very happy to *receive*★ your check for $1,600. It arrived[1] on April 16.

However, there seems to be a discrepancy between the amount of your check and the amount[2] that our records show that you owe us. Our records show that your balance on April 1 was $1,800.[3]

If our records are in error, please let us know. If they are correct, please send us another check for[4] $200.

A stamped, addressed envelope is *enclosed*† for your convenience. Sincerely yours,   [98]

Also correct:
★get, have
†attached

LESSON 32

278 Dear Mrs. Gordon: Thank you for your order for the size 12 dress which was advertised in last Sunday's *Times*. The response[1] to this advertisement was so overwhelming that we sold out all our stock by Tuesday morning.

We will,[2] however, have a new supply sometime next week, and we will send the dress to you just as soon as the shipment arrives.[3] We are confident that when you receive the dress, you will be well rewarded for your patience in waiting for it.[4] You will not, of course, be billed until you receive the dress.

In the next week or two, we will announce another sale[5] of high-quality women's clothing in our regular Sunday advertisement in the *Times*. We suggest that you[6] watch for it and take advantage of the outstanding values it will offer. Very truly yours,   [137]

279 Dear Sir or Madam: Yesterday I received my October telephone bill, and I believe there is an error[1] on it. I was billed $3.50 for a call from my home to Detroit, Michigan, on July 2. I[2] could not have made such a call because on that date I was in Reno, Nevada.

If you will correct and return[3] the enclosed bill to me, I will send you my check in payment. Sincerely yours,   [74]

280 Dear Mr. Troy: You are, of course, right; you should not have been billed for $120 in May. We are[1] certainly aware that errors like this one, which was made in our credit department, do not build goodwill for our[2] organization.

When we received your letter, we investigated the credit charge in question and found the cause[3] of this error.

As you know, your account was established under the name of James C. Troy. We also have an account[4] in the name of James A. Troy. Mr. James A. Troy, who lives at 1145 Main Street in Rochester, New York,[5] purchased a desk from us for $120. This purchase was erroneously charged to your account.[6] We have alerted each of our billing clerks to be extremely careful about such matters in the future. When[7] any credit charge is made in the future, the clerk will double check not only the complete name but also the[8] account number. We want to be sure that you are not subjected to similar inconvenience again.

Please[9] accept our sincere apologies, Mr. Troy. Sincerely yours, [192]

281 Dear Mr. Burns: This letter will confirm our telephone conversation yesterday regarding our order for[1] six calculators.

We understand that you will deliver these calculators to our Chicago office not[2] later than March 18 at a unit price of $120 a machine. The machines are to be[3] shipped by express.

If the above terms agree with your understanding of our telephone conversation, please[4] initial the attached carbon of this letter and return it to me. Very truly yours, [96]

282 Ladies and Gentlemen: People are always ready to write a letter of complaint when they are not satisfied[1] with a product. This letter is different; it is a letter of commendation.

I ordered three boxes of[2] your Christmas cards and sent them to my friends. I have already received letters from a number of them commenting[3] on the beauty of the cards. One friend said she was going to have hers framed!

I know you will be as pleased as I am[4] to learn how many friends liked the cards. Yours very truly, [90]

283 Dear Mr. Crawford: We regret the inconvenience you have been caused by your not receiving the eight dozen[1] towels you ordered on Monday, August 15. I personally traced your order, Mr. Crawford, and found out[2] that these towels were *shipped** to another hotel because of a clerical error in our office. Please accept[3] our sincere apologies for this error. We want to build and maintain your goodwill. We will, of course, do everything[4] in our power to be *certain*† that you receive all future orders on time.

We are today sending you the[5] eight dozen towels by air express; you should have them shortly. Very truly yours, [114]
Also correct:
*sent
†sure

LESSON 33

287 Dear Mr. Webb: Thank you for your order No. 1161 for two Model 240 commercial swivel[1] chairs at $80 each.

Before we ship them, may I tell you about our latest chair, the Model 248.[2] Our engineers have built many novel features and substantial improvements into the new model that are proving[3] to be very popular with business executives. In fact, this new model has been selling so well that[4] we have decided to discontinue the old one as soon as the present stock is depleted.

I would like to[5] suggest that you let us substitute the Model 248 for the Model 240. We know you will like it.[6] The cost is $90, which is only $10 more than the old model. But if you feel you really want[7] the Model 240 chairs, we will be glad to ship them to you; we still have a few left.

Please let us know your wishes[8] on the enclosed postage-paid card. Simply place a check mark in one of the two boxes on the card and mail it[9] to us. We will ship the chairs of your choice without delay. We will await your instructions, Mr. Webb. Sincerely[10] yours,   [201]

288   Dear Mrs. Stevens: Thank you for returning to us the coat on which the dark blue dye ran. Your package arrived some[1] days ago, and we sent the coat to our laboratory in Detroit for a special analysis. When we[2] received the official report from our laboratory supervisor, we learned that some of the dyes used were[3] essentially of poor quality; consequently, we are happy to give you full credit for the coat.

We[4] appreciate your bringing this matter to our attention, Mrs. Stevens. Even the most experienced, successful[5] retailers who exercise the greatest care will occasionally overlook some flaw that should have been[6] discovered. The fact that you brought this to our attention will make us redouble our efforts to see that this does not[7] happen again. Sincerely yours,   [146]

289   Dear Mr. Myers: We were

sorry to learn from your letter of November 15 that the three pieces of luggage[1] we shipped to you had not yet arrived.

We are unable to explain the delay in the delivery of these[2] pieces. Mr. James Brown, manager of our shipping operations, tells me that they left our factory on Wednesday,[3] September 10, by express and that he has a receipt for them initialed by the express company[4] representative. Consequently, you should have had them by this time. We are taking immediate steps to locate[5] the shipment. In the meantime, we are making a duplicate shipment.

We realize that you have been substantially[6] inconvenienced, Mr. Myers, and we apologize. Sincerely yours,   [134]

290   Dear Mr. Parks: Yesterday your truck delivered three executive desks to our Houston depository. These[1] desks were apparently intended to fill our order for three Model 1166 desks which we placed on[2] October 30. If you will refer to that order, you will find that it calls for three of your Model 1156[3] secretarial desks— not three Model 1166 desks.

Please ship us the three desks called for in our order and[4] have your truck pick up the executive desks as we need these desks immediately. Please take care of this exchange[5] without delay. Cordially yours,   [106]

291   Dear Mr. Woods: On Thursday, November 14, we placed an order with you for 12 No. 116 shovels.[1] You told us at the time that this model was out of stock but that you would fill our order by December

10. On[2] December 15, however, you *wrote** us that you were having labor problems in your plant and that you would not[3] be able to ship the shovels *until†* January 3. Here it is January 15, and we have not[4] yet received the shovels.

We feel that we can wait no longer; accordingly, we are placing our order with[5] another supplier.

Please cancel our original order. Sincerely yours,   [114]

Also correct:
*informed
†before

LESSON 34

295 Dear Mr. Woods: We knew that our advertisement in the Sunday, February 21, *Daily Star* featuring[1] a special sale of Johnson tennis rackets would attract a substantial number of customers, but we did not[2] anticipate that the number would be so great. Our entire stock was gone by 10 a.m. on Tuesday, February[3] 23.

Consequently, Mr. Woods, we cannot fill your order for three rackets at this time.[4] However, we are expecting a new shipment of Johnson tennis rackets in about two weeks. If it meets with your[5] approval, we will fill your order from that shipment at the advertised sale price.

When you receive the rackets, we[6] know that you will be rewarded for your patience. Sincerely yours, [132]

296 Dear Mrs. Mason: We are disturbed by your letter telling us that you have not yet received the carpet you purchased[1] from us on Saturday, March 14. The carpet was shipped by express on March 17, and you should have received[2] it a week or ten days ago.

We know that you have been looking forward to enjoying the warmth, beauty, and[3] comfort of this fine carpet in your home, and we regret the delay in delivery. We have asked Mr. Jack White[4] of the United Express Company to find out what caused the delay. At the present time, however, he doesn't[5] have an answer to the problem.

Just as soon as we receive a complete report from him, which should be within[6] ten days, we will get in touch with you. Cordially yours,
[130]

297 Dear Miss Shaw: We were sorry to learn that some of the tools you ordered on April 9 were not included in the[1] shipment you received last week. We make every effort to see that all orders are properly processed, but occasionally[2] an employee doesn't fulfill his or her obligations. The missing implements were shipped yesterday,[3] and you should have them on or before May 1.

We believe you will be interested in a number of new tools[4] which we have added to our line. Will it be convenient for you to see Ms. Gates, our representative in[5] Boston, during the latter part of this month? She would appreciate the opportunity of showing you how[6] these new items will help you increase your company's business and profits.

If there is any way in which we can[7] be of assistance to you in the future, please let us know. Sincerely yours,   [154]

298 Dear Mrs. Simpson: I am sorry

that you had to write us about your order of June 23. Because of[1] some awkward, complicated labor problems that we have had to face, all shipments were held up for a ten-day[2] period. I am happy to say, though, that we are once again on a regular schedule.

We shipped 12 transistor[3] radios to you today; the remaining 13 will be forwarded to you not later than Friday, June 30.[4] We hope, Mrs. Simpson, that this delay in shipment has not caused you any substantial inconvenience.[5] Yours very truly, [104]

299 Dear Mr. Cohen: The information you requested about our calculators is given in the enclosed[1] brochure on pages 18 and 19. There you will find a description of all our models.

May we suggest, Mr.[2] Cohen, that in the future you send any inquiries you may have about our products directly to our[3] New York office. This will enable us to answer your inquiries more promptly. Yours very truly, [78]

300 Dear Ms. Stone: As I am sure you realize, we are disappointed that you have decided to cancel your[1] subscription to the *National Business Bulletin*. We will, of course, comply with your *instructions.**

Your cancellation,[2] however, arrived a little late for us to make a deletion in our computer program in time to stop[3] your July billing. When you receive your July bill, please disregard it.

The *National Business Bulletin* is[4] the finest, most complete magazine of its *type†* on the market today. We hope that in the future we may once[5] again add your name to our list of subscribers. Cordially yours, [112]

Also correct:
*wishes
†kind

LESSON 35

303 Dear Miss Temple: We are quite embarrassed. Yesterday we shipped you a set of green curtains instead of the red ones[1] you wanted. We discovered the error this morning.

It seems that our shipping clerk had orders for two sets of[2] imported curtains to fill—your order for a set of red curtains and another customer's order for a set[3] of green ones. Somehow the orders were confused, and someone in our shipping department sent the green curtains to you[4] and the red ones to the other customer.

Our truck will deliver the correct set to you and pick up the wrong ones[5] within a few days.

We apologize for this error, Miss Temple, and hope that it has not caused you any[6] inconvenience. Yours very truly, [127]

304 Gentlemen: Enclosed is my October statement. On the statement I have marked several purchases that seem to[1] have been included in error. So that I may straighten out the matter promptly, would you please ask someone in your[2] billing department to send me copies of the sales slips for those purchases. Cordially yours, [57]

305 Dear Mrs. Smith: Thank you for your letter of November 5 requesting duplicate copies of all your charge slips.[1] We are enclosing them. You are quite right; the items which you marked on your statement are, of course, not yours. We seemed to[2] have confused your name with that of another customer named Smith, and we included several of her charges[3] on your bill.

Thank you for calling this matter to our attention. We will make a special effort in the future[4] to see that this does not happen again. Sincerely yours, [90]

306 Dear Dr. Palmer: Thank you for writing us about the inconvenience to which you were subjected on your[1] last visit to our sporting goods department. We sincerely regret the deportment of the sales representative[2] who waited on you and apologize for his rudeness.

As you are a long-time charge customer of ours, you[3] know that such conduct on the part of our employees is not customary. We make every effort to select[4] our representatives carefully and to train them to give prompt, courteous service at all times. Being human,[5] however, we occasionally make a mistake and hire someone who fails us.

I assure you, Dr. Palmer,[6] that on your next visit to our store, you will receive service that is prompt, efficient, and courteous. Sincerely[7] yours, [141]

307 Dear Mr. Trent: On August 18 we sent you our order No. 1161 for two gross of your Model[1] 18 pencils.

On August 28 one gross was delivered to us, and we signed a receipt for it. We are[2] wondering what happened to the other gross. Has it been shipped? Is it on back order because you are temporarily[3] out of stock?

We still want the additional gross of pencils provided you can deliver them to us[4] by Friday, September 15. Yours very truly, [90]

308 Dear Ms. Ryan: Your request that we deliver your order for ten portable calculators by December[1] 10 instead of December 15, which is the confirmed date that we gave you, has been referred to me. I wish I[2] could accommodate you, Ms. Ryan, for you have been a good friend of ours for many years.

The delivery date of[3] December 15 was confirmed only after we carefully estimated the time it would take our factory[4] to complete the job. If we were now to move up this date, we might have to disappoint some other customer.[5]

However, I will discuss your request with the production superintendent and see what can be done for you.[6] I will report to you again within a few days. Cordially yours, [133]

309 Dear Miss Best: One of my customers, John H. Brown, told me yesterday that you have a rare coin that you would like to[1] have appraised. He also mentioned that you might be willing to sell it if you were offered a good price.

For more than[2] 20 years I have been buying and selling rare coins. If you would care to bring your coin in the next time you are in[3] the city, I will be glad to appraise it for you. If it is not a duplicate of any of the coins I[4] have in stock, I will be glad to make you a fair offer for it. Sincerely yours, [94]

310 *The Thirteenth Doughnut*

You are probably too young to remember the good old days when the baker gave an extra doughnut to a[1] customer who bought a dozen. That thirteenth doughnut was the baker's way of saying that the customer's business was[2] appreciated. It was a "little extra" that made fast friends.

What does this have to do with office employees?[3] Well, sometimes they have to give the thirteenth doughnut too. They are paid to work a given number of hours a day[4] and to perform definite tasks. But sometimes they have to put forth a little extra effort beyond the call of[5] duty.

When you pitch in during your lunch hour to wind up a rush job, you are giving the thirteenth doughnut. When[6] you go out of your way to win friends for the company for which you work, you are giving the thirteenth doughnut.

When[7] you arrive ten or fifteen minutes before the official starting hour on days that you know will be hectic,[8] you are giving the thirteenth doughnut. And when you stay after closing hours to help get your employer ready[9] for a trip, to wind up an unfinished task, or to help someone else who is working to meet an approaching deadline,[10] you are giving the thirteenth doughnut.

Giving a little extra makes friends for you. It also helps your boss, and[11] what helps your boss almost always helps you. Don't hold back the thirteenth doughnut. Giving more than is expected is part[12] of the philosophy of every secretary who is going places. It means looking on your work as a[13] career, not just as a nine-to-five job that somehow must get done. [272]

CHAPTER 8

LESSON 36

312 Dear Mr. Johnston: Thank you for the check covering my claim for $800 resulting from the accident[1] in which I was involved two weeks ago. The check arrived a few days ago. I want you to know that I[2] appreciate the promptness with which my claim was handled, particularly since the accident occurred outside the[3] United States.

I hope, of course, that I am never again involved in an accident, but if I am, I will[4] have the peace of mind that comes from owning a National policy.

I have told three or four of my friends about[5] the fine service I received from you. I am sure that one or two of them will be applying for National[6] automobile insurance in the future. Cordially yours, [130]

314 Dear Mr. Fox: Congratulations on the arrival of the new addition to your family. This is a[1] wonderful and exciting time for you. However, when the size of your family increases, you are sure to[2] find two conflicting demands on your income. First, you immediately require more money for food, clothing,[3] and medical bills. Second, you need more insurance protection to safeguard your family's future. You will, of[4] course, want to make sure that all these demands are met.

The National Insurance Company has recently devised[5] a combination program of protection that will provide more money for you to use immediately in[6] case of accident or illness. It will at the same time assure you of adequate protection for your family[7] in case of your death. The cost of this plan is about the same as your current life, health, and accident insurance.[8] The increase in the premium should be no more than 5 percent, and I am sure that is well within your budget.[9]

Let us send one of our representatives to tell you about this new plan, Mr. Fox. Sincerely yours,   [199]

315 Dear Mr. Hunter: If a major fire closed down your business for a month, would you ever get back into business?[1] As many studies have proved, over 50 percent of the businesses that burn down never reopen. It is[2] a sad fact, but it is true. Without a steady flow of new income, it is difficult for a business to survive.[3]

But you can protect yourself by purchasing business interruption insurance, which provides the income you[4] would normally receive. This insurance can be tailored specifically to meet your exact requirements as part[5] of a commercial insurance package policy.

Why not arrange an appointment with one of our experienced,[6] well-trained representatives to learn more about this business interruption insurance. This step may one day[7] save your business. Very truly yours,   [147]

316 Dear Mr. Henry: Enclosed is a

plan that we are sure is the finest ever offered in the field of business[1] insurance. Study it carefully. See if it meets the needs of your organization for full protection from[2] fire, accident, and other catastrophes.

On Monday, February 3, our representative, Mrs. Jane Becker,[3] will call at your office to discuss this plan with you and to give any further explanation of it that[4] you may desire.

In keeping with your recent expansion program, you will surely be purchasing more trucks to meet[5] your growing needs. Let us be the underwriters for all your future automotive insurance as well. When Mrs.[6] Becker calls, she will gladly discuss the savings you will be able to make by having us handle your[7] insurance. Yours truly,   [144]

317 Dear Mr. Black: This letter contains an urgent message that requires your immediate attention, Mr. Black.[1] If we do not *receive** your payment of $50 by March 14, we will have to cancel your insurance[2] policy.

Don't make it necessary for us to take this action; its consequences are too serious. We[3] have seen much unhappiness result from the failure of a father to keep up the payments on his policy.[4]

You will find enclosed a stamped, self-addressed envelope. Please use it to send us your *check*† for $50 without[5] delay. Sincerely yours,   [104]

Also correct:
*have
†payment

322 Dear Mr. Hunt: If you are like most business executives, you probably think that you have enough insurance[1] to meet today's responsibilities. Suppose, however, that in a few years you have one or two children and[2] find that you need more coverage. What will happen if you cannot get it because you cannot pass the necessary[3] medical examination?

We here at the United Insurance Company of America have[4] seen this happen many times. It can happen to you. That is why it is particularly important that you[5] speak with one of our well-trained representatives without delay. Mr. James Short is the representative assigned[6] to your area; he knows the difficulties a young family may have to face. Why not request him to[7] call on you soon. When he visits you, he will suggest several plans to meet your present and future needs. His[8] suggestions may safeguard the future happiness of your family, but his call will place you under no obligation.[9] Yours very truly,   [184]

323 Gentlemen: I cannot let another day go by without writing to your executive office about my[1] experience with one of your representatives, Mr. John C. Worth.

While my son and I were on vacation,[2] we were driving on Route 16 near Juneau, Alaska. We had a very bad accident in which, fortunately,[3] both of us were only slightly injured. It could easily have been a fatal accident.

As soon as I[4] called your office in Juneau, Mr. Worth got into his car and drove 30 miles from his home to the scene of the[5] accident. He took a deep, personal interest in our situation and did not leave the scene of the[6] accident until the situation was under control. After we returned to our home here in Wyoming, we[7] had a personal note from him.

We are grateful for Mr. Worth's help. He is a great asset to your organization.[8] Sincerely yours,   [164]

324 Dear Miss King: Group dental insurance is becoming more and more popular as a fringe benefit in many[1] organizations. You, too, may soon want to consider it for your employees. When you are ready to do this,[2] take advantage of the experience of the Mutual Insurance Company, which serves every state in the Union[3] including Alaska and Hawaii. We were one of the first companies to offer this type of insurance,[4] and we can help you set up a program that will provide the maximum benefits for your employees at[5] the minimum expense to you.

Talk to one of our agents and find out about the specific advantages[6] of letting us handle your group dental insurance. You will be placing yourself under no obligation by[7] doing so. Cordially yours,   [145]

325 Dear Ms. Ward: As you have perhaps read in the newspapers, I have just been appointed to the staff of Mayor Green.[1] This makes it necessary for me to divest myself of my interest in the American Insurance[2] Company.

Beginning April 1, I am turning over the agency to Mr. Harry H. Miller, who[3] has been in the insurance business for more than 20 years. He is in a position to help you with any[4] problems you may have.

Mr. Miller will administer the agency from his office at 1116 Fifth[5] Avenue in St. Louis, Missouri. Please address all communications to him at that address.

Thank you, Ms.[6] Ward, for the confidence you have placed in me by entrusting your insurance business to me during the past six[7] years. Sincerely yours,   [144]

326 Dear Mr. Smith: We at the Mutual Insurance Company believe that people who don't smoke make better insurance[1] risks than those who do. Consequently, we give them a better insurance rate.

If you haven't smoked cigarettes[2] in at least a year, you qualify for one of our special policies that save you up to 5 percent of the[3] usual premium.

If you do not smoke, investigate the savings you can make with one of our policies. We[4] will be glad to give you complete information if you will fill out and return the enclosed card. Sincerely yours,[5]   [100]

327 Dear Miss Smith: Enclosed is a folder that describes a number of our new services to the public. Because you[1] are already aware of the benefits to which you are entitled as an automobile insurance[2] policyholder, we are sure you will want to know about our other reliable services. Sincerely yours,[3]   [60]

328 Dear Mr. Kelly: Enclosed is your new insurance policy. It consists of two pages, and they should be kept[1] together as evidence of

your airline insurance coverage.

Please check the information printed by the[2] computer on the first page of your policy to be sure that it is accurate. If all the *information**[3] is not accurate, please let us know immediately.

By this time, Mr. Kelly, you should have received the summer[4] issue of *American Aviation News*, the magazine sent free to all our policyholders. I[5] hope you take the time to read the fine *articles*† it contains. I am sure you will find them informative, enlightening,[6] and entertaining. Sincerely yours,   [128]
Also correct:
*data
†material

LESSON 38

332 Dear Mr. Boyd: Good wholesale customers can become financial problems almost overnight. The profits of their[1] businesses may drop, their overhead may rise, or their customers may be negligent in paying their bills. This can[2] result in bankruptcy for your wholesale customers. Suddenly your customers' critical problems become your[3] critical problems.

You can guard against this situation, however, by purchasing business credit insurance.[4] When one of your customers becomes bankrupt, this insurance protects you.

Learn all about this valuable[5] insurance by reading our booklet, *Protection From Credit Losses*; it is enclosed.

After you have read it, invite[6] one of our experienced, well-trained agents to tell you how credit insurance can protect your accounts receivable.[7] Sincerely yours,   [144]

333 Dear Mr. Hicks: Many insurance companies feel that they have served a client well if they have paid a loss claim[1] quickly.

At the American Insurance Company, however, we feel that we owe much more to our clients.[2] We want to assist them in keeping losses from happening in the first place. In fact, we maintain a special[3] loss-prevention department consisting of 200 people. These people inspect and appraise properties, and they[4] develop standards for approved loss-preventive devices. They probe into the causes and control of fires,[5] explosions, and other losses.

Let us tell you about our services. One of our agents will be glad to call on[6] you at your convenience. All that is necessary to arrange an interview is a call to[7] 555-1818. Sincerely yours,   [146]

334 Dear Mr. Clark: Suppose your mother, father, or some other relative over sixty-five became ill and[1] required urgent medical or surgical assistance. Would you have the means to provide it? You would if you subscribed[2] to our special hospital plan for senior citizens.

This plan, which is described in the enclosed booklet, is[3] a very popular form of insurance. Many senior citizens throughout the country use it to supplement[4] their medicare benefits. If there is someone near and dear to you who needs additional protection against[5] constantly rising health costs, this plan is a perfect solution.

May I have a few minutes of your time, Mr.[6] Clark, to discuss this plan with you? My visit will place you under no obligation. Cordially yours,   [138]

335 Dear Mrs. Yale: If your son were critically injured by a motor vehicle while riding his bicycle to[1] school, would you be able to take care of his medical bills? You would be able to do so if you had provided[2] for his protection with one of our medical insurance policies. These policies are designed for school[3] children five years of age and over. Various insurance combinations, all of which are described in the enclosed[4] leaflet, are available.

Before the next school term begins, give your child the protection of one of our[5] policies. It could save you a great deal of money in the future. Yours very truly,   [115]

336 Dear Mr. Meade: Your company works hard for its profits. It is only proper, therefore, that you protect them. We[1] can help you do this.

We are the world's largest organization of insurance consultants. With our capabilities[2] we will look after your profits in a wide range of ways. We will tailor your insurance program to your[3] company's own special problems. We will help you cut the costs of your employees' benefits. We will help your[4] treasurer choose the best investments for your pension fund.

Today Wilson Associates is protecting the profits[5] of hundreds of organizations. May we tell you how we can protect yours? Sincerely yours,   [117]

337 Dear Mr. Fenton: Who will

pay the family's bills if you should become disabled? It takes a regular income[1] to keep a family running smoothly. That is why a National disability income policy can[2] come in handy if sickness or injury prevents you from bringing home your regular paycheck.

This policy[3] provides a regular monthly income to help you meet family expenses like rent, food, and clothing.

Being[4] disabled is not pleasant to think about, but everyone must face the possibility.

So if you are not[5] covered for disability, ask to see one of our agents today. Our agent will help you plan the policy[6] that is just right for your family. Our number is (800) 411-1161. Sincerely yours,[7]   [140]

338 Dear Mr. Nelson: The enclosed envelope contains your policy No. 11811. We are sure it[1] will *bring** you the peace of mind that comes with the knowledge that you have made provision for your family should anything[2] happen to you. As I am sure you *realize,*† your policy is a valuable document. Keep it in[3] a safe place.

All official records pertaining to your policy are kept in our St. Louis office. Should you[4] wish any information about your policy, please write or call that office.

Thank you, Mr. Nelson, for[5] entrusting your insurance needs to us. Sincerely yours,   [110]
Also correct:
*give
†know

LESSON 39

342 Dear Mr. Blair: If your business partner should pass away, could you get along with his relatives? The loss of a[1] business partner might ultimately result in exceedingly difficult circumstances.

If you do not have[2] the necessary cash to purchase your partner's share from his heirs, you may have a very difficult time. The heirs[3] might not willingly sit back and let you run the business yourself. You may know you can run the business better than[4] they, but do they realize it themselves?

You can circumvent this problem, Mr. Blair, with the help of business life[5] insurance. This type of insurance can provide you the cash necessary to buy the shares owned by a deceased[6] partner.

Talk this matter over with one of our insurance supervisors. When you do, you will be placing yourself[7] under no obligation. Sincerely yours,   [149]

343 Dear Ms. Dunn: Let us suppose that you and your partner have worked long and diligently to make your business a success,[1] but suddenly your partner died. Would you be able to adjust? Who would inherit your partner's share? How much[2] would his loss affect your business?

The Superior Life Insurance Company can make it a lot easier[3] for you to answer these questions. Here is how.

You and your partner should sign a buy-sell agreement now and fund it[4] with National life insurance. If your partner dies, you are guaranteed the right to buy his share in the business,[5] and we will provide the cash.

This insurance protects your family too. If you should die, your partner has the cash[6] to buy your share in the business from your heirs at a fair price.

Let Mr. William Jones, our business insurance[7] specialist, explain the plan to you in detail. He has had ten years' experience in providing business insurance[8] to executives in this area. There is no one in the state better qualified than he to evaluate[9] your insurance needs. Let him show you how surprisingly inexpensive business insurance is. Tell us[10] on the enclosed card when he may call. Yours very truly,   [210]

344   Dear Miss Mills: Your business may seemingly be having a great year. But suddenly a partner, a key supervisor,[1] or a superintendent dies. Can your business survive under those circumstances? It can if you have business[2] life insurance.

Business life insurance will do three things for you:

1. It will keep your business going without[3] interruption.

2. It will help assure the future stability of your business.

3. It will help you hold[4] talented employees.

If you want accurate, detailed information on how business life insurance can be made[5] to work for you, call us at 555-1181. We will send one of our supervisors to your office[6] at your convenience. Sincerely yours,   [127]

345   Dear Mr. Hansen: Please do

me a favor. As you know, on Wednesday, November 16, you permitted life[1] insurance policy No. 11851 to lapse. I would like to know why you let this happen.

I realize,[2] of course, that this request is of a very personal nature; therefore, I am enclosing a stamped, self-addressed[3] envelope marked "Confidential." It will come directly to my desk.

You are, I know, very busy at this[4] time of the year, but do take a few minutes to give me this information. When I know the exact reasons for[5] your action, perhaps I can make some constructive suggestions on how you can replace this valuable protection.[6] Your answer may mean a great deal for the future protection of your family. Sincerely yours, [137]

346   Dear Mr. Andrews: I appreciate your offer to discuss my insurance program with me. My assistant,[1] whose insurance you have handled for several years, speaks very highly of your *company** and of you personally.[2]

I should tell you, however, that my insurance needs have been handled by Mr. Sam Martin of the[3] Superior Insurance Company for the past ten years, and he has always given me superior service.[4] Under the circumstances, I feel that he is entitled to my loyalty. You probably have many clients[5] who feel equally loyal to you.

While I cannot take advantage of your offer to serve my insurance[6] needs, I will be *delighted*† to meet you socially. Sincerely yours,   [133]
Also correct:
*organization
†happy, glad

LESSON 40

349 Dear Miss Arnold: Would you like to have a copy of the deluxe *Ideal World Atlas* with our compliments? A[1] copy is yours if you will fill in the information called for on the enclosed card and return it to us.

When[2] we receive it, we will send you the atlas and also a copy of a manual that is of value to[3] everyone who owns life insurance. It is called *The Guide to Term Life Insurance*. It gives important information[4] about term life insurance and how you can make it function to take care of your needs.

Return the card today,[5] Miss Arnold. The atlas and manual will be on their way to you shortly after we receive the card. Very[6] truly yours,

[122]

350 Dear Mr. Dixon: Selecting the right life insurance company for yourself or for your employees' benefit[1] program is a serious, complex, and taxing chore. Just how do you determine which company to choose?

You[2] could talk with a representative of every life insurance company in the area. That would take a[3] long time, however; there are over 100 of them.

A much simpler, quicker way is to read our informative[4] booklet on how to select a life insurance company. The booklet, which is written mainly for the[5] layman, will also help those involved in the process of choosing an insurance company for their group life, health,[6] and profit-sharing plans. It won't make you an expert, but it will give you enough basic knowledge so that you can[7] make a wise decision.

If you would like a copy of this booklet, mail the coupon that is enclosed. We will send[8] you one with our compliments. Sincerely yours,

[168]

351 Dear Mr. Cohen: On Thursday, December 18, my daughter broke the news to her mother and me that she was[1] going to be married. Frankly, this didn't surprise us. We had known the fine young man to whom she is engaged for[2] a period of three years.

The selection of an ideal wedding gift for the couple wasn't any problem.[3] Many years ago my wife and I decided that we would give each of our children a life insurance[4] policy as a wedding gift and that we would pay the first five years' premiums in advance. This worthwhile gift will give[5] the couple five years in which these premiums will not have to be included in their budget. By the end of the[6] fifth year, that insurance will be far too valuable for them to let it lapse.

For many years your company has[7] taken care of our insurance needs, and we have nothing but praise for the high quality of your service. The[8] application for a life insurance policy for my daughter and future son-in-law is enclosed. Sincerely[9] yours, [181]

352 Dear Mrs. Franklin: On behalf of the board of directors and officers of the National Insurance[1] Company, may I express to you our appreciation for your friendship and business.

As you know, you purchased your[2] first insurance policy from us on Friday, January 2, 1975, and since then you have[3] purchased additional insurance several times.

Our representative in your territory, Miss Myra[4] Nelson, tells us that you have said some complimentary things about us to your friends and that a number of them[5] have purchased policies from us. Thank you, Mrs. Franklin, for your efforts on our behalf.

If you are ever in[6] Hartford, please stop in to see us. It will be a genuine pleasure to meet you personally. Sincerely yours,[7]   [140]

353 Dear Mrs. Barnes: As a service to the public, we have recently published a 64-page booklet on life[1] insurance. A copy is yours for the asking. It answers many frequently asked questions about life insurance[2] in plain, easy-to-understand language. No doubt it contains the answers to many questions you may have about[3] life insurance. To obtain a copy, simply mail the enclosed card; it requires no postage. By sending for[4] the booklet, you will assume no obligation, nor will a representative call unless you request us to[5] send one. Sincerely yours,
[104]

354 *Why Mildred Anderson Lost Her Job*

On Monday, Mildred Anderson was given an assignment and told by her employer, "This should be on my desk[1] no later than next Monday at nine. If you need any help, let me know, but don't wait until Friday to tell me[2] about it."

Mildred felt confident that she would have no difficulty meeting that deadline so she kept putting[3] the assignment off. Procrastination was her middle name. She postponed the work for so long that at 4 o'clock[4] on Friday she realized she could not make the deadline.

Since she had an important social date at 5:30,[5] she decided to wait until Monday morning, expecting to come in early to get the job done.

Do you think[6] she finished the job on time for her employer? She did not. Her employer asked why she had not asked for help. Her answer[7] was typical of many she had given before: "I thought I could get it done on time."

The employer[8] told her he felt the job was too much for her. He said he just didn't have the time to be constantly checking[9] everything she did. He said, further, that he felt they would both be happier if she looked for another job. He gave[10] her two weeks' notice and told her that she could use part of a few days to look for another job.

Perhaps you think[11] he was acting hastily about this. No, Mildred had done countless things which indicated that she either was[12] not interested in the job or that it truly was too much for her. Here are just a few of the things that happened[13] before the Monday episode:

She sent a package to Portland, Oregon, instead of Portland, Maine.

She forgot[14] to write down an important telephone message.

She made a typographical error on an expense report.[15]

She made three long-distance, personal calls on the company phone during working hours.

She forgot to put an[16] important meeting on the calendar.

So, failure to have the assignment on her employer's desk by nine on[17] that particular Monday morning was the last straw.   [350]

PART

Chapters 9-12
Lessons 41-60

CHAPTER 9

LESSON 41

356 Dear Mrs. Jones: I am sending you separately a complete set of the drawings I have prepared for the new[1] book you are publishing, *Making Things With Your Hands*. As you are aware, I have spent several months working on these[2] illustrations, and I hope you will be pleased with them.

There are three drawings for each one of the chapters in the book.[3] As you suggested, I have done each one of them in three colors. If you want me to make any changes in the[4] drawings, please let me know as soon as possible. I will, of course, be glad to make any changes you wish. Sincerely[5] yours,   [101]

359 Dear Mr. Stern: Here is your copy of our new history textbook, *Your Country and Mine*, by Dr. Lee R. Keith.[1] I believe you will agree that it is one of the most beautiful history texts ever published.

Please notice[2] especially Chapter 9, "The Civil War." Dr. Keith has included in this chapter the latest findings[3] about the causes and results of the Civil War. Also included in this chapter are copies of some of the[4] best, most beautiful paintings from the Civil War era.

We hope you will consider *Your Country and Mine* for your[5] students for the next school year. If you would like to order copies for your classes, just fill out the enclosed order[6] blank and return it in the postage-paid envelope that we have provided. Cordially yours,   [137]

360 Gentlemen: As your records will show, several months ago we ordered 100 copies of the high school textbook,[1] *Science and You*. The books arrived during the summer, and we thought that we would have an ample supply for[2] several terms. When I returned to school in September, I found this was not the case. We had approximately[3] twice as many students as we expected.

We will, therefore, need an additional 100 copies of the[4] text immediately. Will you please send these books to us as soon as possible. Thank you for your help. Very truly[5] yours,   [101]

361 Dear Miss Carter: Thank you for your letter concerning your order for 100 copies of the book, *Science and[1] You*. We are delighted that you are using the text in your classes this year.

We are sending you immediately[2] 100 more copies of the book, and you should have them by the end of the week.

If we can be of further[3] help to you, I hope you will let us know; we are here to serve our customers' needs. Sincerely yours,   [77]

362 Ladies and Gentlemen: For the past three years I have been receiving your publication, *The Home Magazine*, on[1] a regular basis. Several months ago I missed an issue of the magazine, and I did nothing about[2] it. The following month I received my copy on time. But this month the magazine arrived nearly three weeks[3] late. Frankly, I am perturbed.

Please check into the matter immediately to see what the problem could be. I[4] would like to keep my subscription. However, I want to get all of the magazines, and I want to get them on[5] time. Sincerely yours, [104]

363 Dear Ms. Chang: Thank you for writing to us about the problem you have had receiving our publication, *The Home*[1] *Magazine*. I am certainly sorry that you have not had satisfactory service.

I checked into the matter[2] myself, Ms. Chang, and found that your copy has been sent to you on time each month from our main office. I am afraid,[3] therefore, that the problem is with the postal service. We are checking into this matter now.

In the future[4] if you do not get your copy of *The Home Magazine* on time, please use one of the enclosed cards to notify[5] us. We will then send you another copy immediately. Thank you for your patience. Sincerely yours, [118]

364 Gentlemen: I would like to order several copies of your magazine, *Children's World*, to use as Christmas gifts.[1] On the enclosed sheet there are names and addresses of five boys and girls to whom I would like to send subscriptions. Will[2] you please start these subscriptions with the December issue and continue sending them monthly during the coming[3] year.

I will send you a check as soon as I receive your statement. Sincerely yours, [74]

365 Dear Bill: The children received their first copy of the magazine, *Children's World*, in the mail today. Thank you very[1] much for the subscription; it is certainly a wonderful Christmas gift.

The children were too excited for words.[2] Each of them read every story. They particularly *liked** the stories about the way Christmas is[3] celebrated in Spain, France, and Germany. They are already looking forward to receiving next month's issue.

The children[4] are both writing you letters, but I wanted to tell you how much I personally appreciate your[5] thoughtfulness.

Best wishes to you, Bill, for a very *happy†* Christmas. Sincerely yours, [115]

Also correct:
*enjoyed
†merry, wonderful

LESSON 42

370 Dear Mr. Underwood: I have recently become interested in business correspondence, and I hope[1] to introduce a short, intensive course in the subject at the Philadelphia Business College next spring.[2] I have conferred with Dr. Jane Washington, dean of the evening school, about this idea and she likes it[3] very much.

Dr. Washington has consented to place the course on the spring schedule, and if there is sufficient[4] enrollment, I will begin teaching the first week in February.

I now need to find a good textbook on[5] general business correspondence to use in the course. Does your company publish such a book? If you have a[6] text to suggest, I would appreciate hearing from you. I will be at my home in Trenton, New Jersey, until[7] Monday, January

5. Sincerely yours,   [148]

371 Dear Mrs. Overmeyer: We are very happy to hear that you are planning to teach a course in business[1] correspondence at the Philadelphia Business College next semester. We believe that this course will serve a real[2] need.

We do indeed have a very good book on business correspondence entitled *Business Communications*.[3] It was written by Dr. Lee Smith, associate professor at California University, and[4] Dr. Paul Miller, professor emeritus of Pennsylvania College. We are sending you a copy of the[5] book separately; you should have it in a few days.

The text contains five major sections divided into ten[6] chapters. The introductory chapter is on the subject of business psychology. It includes discussions[7] on how business may be won or lost through the correspondence which a company sends out. I think you will like this[8] chapter in particular.

I hope, Mrs. Overmeyer, that you will find *Business Communications* to be[9] just the book you need for your course. When you have had an opportunity to study the book, I hope you will[10] decide to use it next spring. Cordially yours,   [207]

372 Dear Ms. Sweet: We are happy to announce the publication of the new edition of the *General Atlas*[1] *of the United States*. This book, which came off the press on October 15, is not an ordinary road atlas.[2] Of course, it contains the usual detailed maps of all the states. In addition, it includes large, easy-to-read[3] maps of New York, Chicago, and 25 other major cities.

It also contains listings of the best[4] restaurants in each state, the best hotels and motels in each area, and the leading radio and television[5] stations in every major city. Altogether, the atlas contains over 1,000 pages[6] of reliable, up-to-date information that every traveler needs.

If you have seen a copy, you[7] have probably ordered one for yourself by this time. If you have not seen one, I would like to send you a copy for[8] a free ten-day review. After ten days if you are convinced that it is the best atlas on the market today,[9] just send us a check for $12.

If, however, you decide not to keep the atlas, just return it to us[10] at our expense. Fill out the attached order card today and mail it to us in the enclosed self-addressed envelope.[11] Sincerely yours,   [224]

373 Dear Mr. Torres: I would like to order one copy of the *General Atlas of the United States*. I[1] understand that the volume sells for $12. I am enclosing a check for this amount plus the 5 percent[2] sales tax regularly charged in the state of New Jersey.

Because I will want to consult this book in planning a[3] trip I have to make in the next few weeks, I hope you will send it to me without delay. Cordially yours,   [78]

374 Dear Sir: I will be attending the annual convention of the Pennsylvania Publishing Association[1] which is being held in Pittsburgh this year, and I would like to make a reservation at your hotel.

Will[2] you please reserve a single room for me for the nights of Sunday, Monday, and Tuesday, August 3, 4, and 5. Please[3] mark the reservation for late arrival. Also, please confirm this reservation. Yours truly, [77]

375 Dear Ms. Stern: We are happy to confirm your reservation at the Hotel President in Pittsburgh, Pennsylvania,[1] for the nights of Sunday, Monday, and Tuesday, August 3, 4, and 5. The rate will be $20 a[2] day, our hotel's lowest convention rate. As you requested, we will hold the room for late arrival.

We are looking[3] forward to having you with us during the convention of the Pennsylvania Publishing Association.[4] Cordially yours, [83]

376 Dear Dr. Cunningham: In three months my secretary, Ms. Diana Morris, will be moving to England, and[1] I will need someone to replace her at that time. If you know of anyone you think might be able to handle[2] this job, I hope you will let me know.

I need a *person** who has a strong background in English and who can type and[3] take shorthand. Some experience in the publishing field would be helpful, but it is not essential. The person[4] must be someone who can assume a great deal of responsibility and who can work with very little[5] supervision.

If you have someone you can *recommend*,† please ask the person to call me as soon as possible. Thank[6] you for your help. Very truly yours, [127]

Also correct:
*worker, man or woman
†suggest

LESSON 43

380 Dear Friends: The purpose of this letter is to introduce our new book on computer programming and operation,[1] *Computers Now*. The book describes the functions of computer input and output. It discusses fully the[2] principles of data storage and retrieval. I think you will find it to be the most modern, complete book on[3] computer programming ever written.

The reading level is well within reach of almost any college[4] student, and the examples are amply illustrated. If you would like to have a copy of *Computers Now*, just[5] fill out and return the enclosed card. We will send you a copy by return mail. Cordially yours, [117]

381 Dear Dr. Sloan: Here is your copy of our new textbook, *Computers Now*. Please look through it at your convenience. I[1] hope you will pay particular attention to the section on computer languages. There is a separate[2] chapter on each of the languages in common use in business today. In addition to the textbook, we have[3] available a teacher's handbook and a student's workbook.

I am confident you will agree with us that[4] *Computers Now* is the best, most comprehensive book on computers in the field today. If you should decide to use[5] the book in your classes, we will be glad to fill your order promptly. The book sells for $8 from which you may[6] deduct your usual school discount. Sincerely yours, [130]

382 Dear Miss Poland: Enclosed is an outline for a new textbook I plan to write. Will you please study the outline and[1] let me know if you think your company would be interested in publishing it.

As you will see, the book is[2] about the role of women in business today. I believe that this is a very timely subject which will[3] interest a large number of people. If you like the ideas listed in the outline, I can prepare a[4] preliminary manuscript in about six months. Yours very truly, [93]

383 Dear Mr. Hastings: Three years ago I subscribed to your series of children's books for my son Kenneth. At that time[1] he was five years old. We chose the primary series on life in the country. He has enjoyed reading all of the[2] books, but he is now ready to move ahead to more advanced books. We would, therefore, like to discontinue our[3] subscription to the primary series and begin receiving books on the intermediate level.

Will you please[4] send me a catalog of the books you have which would be of interest and at the proper grade level for an[5] eight-year-old child. He will be completing the third grade this spring.

When I receive the catalog, I will let him choose[6] the series he wants to read. Sincerely yours, [128]

384 Dear Mr. Morris: Thank you for your letter asking about our intermediate books for children. We have[1] several sets of books which are designed for children at this level. They are all fully described in the enclosed[2] catalog.

We will begin sending you the books that your son prefers just as soon as we receive your order.

We are[3] very happy that your son enjoyed the basic reading books, Mr. Morris, and we are confident that he will[4] not be disappointed in the advanced books. Sincerely yours, [91]

385 Dear Miss Barry: Congratulations on your graduation from the Nelson School of Management. I know this[1] represents a milestone in your career. Today more and more women are taking their places in the field of management,[2] and I am sure you are on your way to accepting a desirable position in business today.

All[3] well-informed business executives must keep up with the latest developments affecting the field of management.[4] That is why we publish *The Management Guide*.

The Management Guide is the most complete, comprehensive, and[5] up-to-date magazine in the field today. We want you to have a free subscription for a period of three months[6] so that you can discover for yourself how valuable it is. After that time, we are sure you will want to[7] subscribe to it. Look for your first copy in the mail in the next few days. Cordially yours, [156]

386 Dear Ms. Dix: Since the beginning of the year, I have been *receiving** complimentary copies of your magazine,[1] *The Management Guide*. I enjoyed reading some of the articles, but I was disappointed in the magazine[2] in general. Therefore, I decided not to subscribe.

In the mail today I was dismayed to find the[3] latest issue along with a bill for the coming year. I understood, Ms. Dix, that I would not receive a bill for[4] the copies unless I subscribed to the magazine.

Please *correct*† your records and take my name off your mailing list.[5] Sincerely yours, [103]

Also correct:

*getting

†check

LESSON 44

390 Dear Miss Flowers: In just a few weeks' time you will be selecting Christmas gifts for your family and friends. Have you[1] given thought to what you would like to give them this year? If you haven't, here is a suggestion: Give them a subscription[2] to one of their favorite magazines.

I am enclosing a complete list of our periodicals. I[3] know you will find something just right for everyone on your Christmas list. I am also enclosing an order[4] form. Just fill it out according to the directions. Then each month we will send the magazines directly to your[5] family and friends.

Give your family and friends a gift that will remind them of you every month of the new[6] year; give them a magazine subscription. Cordially yours, [130]

391 Dear Miss Flowers: Thank you for your order for five 1-year magazine subscriptions to be sent as Christmas gifts. We[1] have processed your order following your directions precisely, and the people on your list will begin receiving[2] their magazines shortly after December 1.

Our bill, which covers a complete year for all five magazines,[3] is enclosed. We know that you will be remembered all year for your thought-

fulness, Miss Flowers. Yours very truly, [79]

392 Dear Dr. Mason: I am sending you separately a complete set of the proofs of your book on medical[1] office procedures. Will you please read them carefully and let us know if there are any changes you would like made[2] before we order the books to be printed. However, please do not make any changes that will affect the size[3] of the book.

I have read the proofs carefully. As you can see, the typesetter has done an exceptional job. There[4] are a few errors which I have marked; they can be easily corrected.

Please return the proofs to us before the[5] end of the month. Sincerely yours, [106]

393 Dear Mrs. Case: I just received the proofs of my new book, and I will begin reading them immediately. I[1] took a few minutes to look through the proofs, and I agree with you that the typesetter has done an exceptional[2] job.

I will return the marked set just as soon as I have finished reading it. Yours very truly, [57]

394 Dear Mr. Wilson: I have been named program chairman for the national convention of the American[1] Publishing Association, and I would like to ask you to be on our program. The convention will be held on[2] Wednesday, Thursday, and Friday, September 4, 5, and 6, next year in Chicago, Illinois. I would like you[3] to make the opening speech at the first session on September 4. You may, of course, speak on any topic in[4] the field of publishing. I hope, though, you will discuss the effect of governmental regulation on the[5] publishing industry.

Please let me know as soon as possible if you can accept this invitation. Cordially[6] yours, [121]

395 Dear Ms. Larson: Thank you very much for the kind invitation to speak at the opening session of next year's[1] convention of the American Publishing Association on Wednesday, September 4. I am[2] happy to accept. I will speak on the ways government regulations affect the publishing industry.

When you[3] have additional information about the convention such as the name of the hotel where the meeting will[4] be held, the size of the audience you expect, and the time of the meeting, please send it to me. Cordially yours,[5] [100]

396 Dear Mr. Best: It is with regret that I must tell you that we have stopped publishing our monthly bulletin,[1] *Insurance Notes.* Increasing costs of printing and postage have made it necessary for us to cease publishing[2] after 36 years of service. We will use the services of our staff in other areas where they are[3] sorely needed.

We deeply appreciate the many letters we have received from our readers telling us how much[4] they enjoyed *Insurance Notes* and profited from its suggestions.

We hope that whenever you have insurance[5] problems with which a representative of ours can help you, you will not hesitate to call us, Mr. Best. Our[6] telephone number is 116-1181. Sincerely yours, [132]

397 Dear Mr. Hastings: The sales staff of my organization, the General Publishing Company, will be[1] holding its annual marketing meeting on October 3, 4, and 5 next year, and we are looking for a good[2] place to hold the meeting. I would like to have information about the facilities your hotel has to[3] offer for meetings of this type.

We have approximately 150 sales representatives, and we will[4] *need**
a large meeting room for general sessions as well as several smaller meeting rooms for special programs.[5] We will also need guest rooms for each of the representatives for three nights. Because our time is limited, we[6] will need to have our meals catered.

If your hotel can handle this *type†* of meeting, please send us information[7] about your facilities. Sincerely yours, [147]
Also correct:
*require
†kind, size

LESSON 45

400 Dear Miss Keith: Thank you very much for your invitation to speak at the annual meeting of the American[1] Publishing Club this fall. I am pleased to accept.

If it is satisfactory with you, I will speak on the[2] topic "Improving Your Writing Style."

Please make arrangements for me to have a lapel microphone, an overhead[3] projector, and a screen. I will bring several transparencies to use during the speech and several booklets[4] for the members of the audience.

As soon as I have made my travel arrangements, I will let you know

the time[5] and place of my arrival.
Sincerely yours, [108]

401 Dear Dr. Black: The members of the American Publishing Club are delighted that you will be able to[1] speak at our annual meeting this fall on November 13. The topic suggested, "Improving Your Writing[2] Style," is an excellent one.

We have made arrangements for you to stay in the Hotel Brown, which is near the[3] auditorium where you will be speaking. There will be a lapel microphone, an overhead projector, and a screen[4] for your use during the talk. If there is anything else that you will need, just let us know.

As I wrote you in my[5] previous letter, we will arrange to have someone meet your plane if you will let us know which flight you plan to take.[6] We are looking forward to your visit. Sincerely yours, [130]

402 Dear Dr. Black: Thank you very much for the wonderful talk you made to our publishing organization last[1] week. All the members agreed that it was a splendid, thought-provoking speech. In fact, many of the members stated[2] that it was by far the best program we have had this year.

I am enclosing a small honorarium; please[3] accept it with our compliments. I hope, Dr. Black, that you will be able to speak to our organization[4] again in the near future. We would like that very much. Sincerely yours, [93]

403 Dear Mr. Quill: It has been a pleasure during the past year to bring you all the local news in your

copy of[1] Trenton's leading newspaper, the *Daily News*.

On Monday, June 15, we will celebrate your first anniversary[2] as a subscriber. The subscription might seem a small matter to you, but to us it represents a one-family[3] increase in our circulation. And our future success depends on our getting and holding new subscribers.[4]

Although we now have over 50,000 daily readers, we are happy only if we satisfy each[5] and every one.

Thank you for your loyalty during the past year. As a token of our appreciation,[6] you will receive your subscription to the *Daily News* free for one month beginning June 15. Cordially yours, [139]

404 Dear Friend: Apartment dwellers are hard to reach. The superintendent of an apartment building usually[1] frowns on people who come to the door to sell anything. And when you consider how much time this has saved you, you[2] are probably very glad.

But this isolation also puts you beyond the reach of much local news. You miss[3] news of civic clubs, service organizations, and houses of worship.

If you would like to keep up with all the[4] events in your neighborhood but do not want sales representatives pounding on your door daily, why not subscribe[5] to the *Daily News*. For only a few cents a day, you can be as well informed as the local mayor.

Just fill[6] out and return the enclosed card; your subscription will begin the day after we receive your order. Sincerely[7] yours, [141]

405 *The Person Who Never Makes a Mistake*

A business executive recently said to a new stenographer, "Why didn't you go ahead with this[1] job?" The stenographer answered, "I was afraid I might make a mistake." The executive then told the secretary,[2] "The biggest mistake is to feel that you'll make one."

There are mistakes that are due to lack of experience[3] or judgment. These mistakes will become fewer and fewer with experience if you really care to learn. If you[4] are given some authority to try certain assignments, do everything you can to check procedure in an[5] office manual, reference books, or in the files. Then try to do *something* rather than nothing. It might mean asking[6] questions of your employer or others who "know the ropes." As you acquire more experience, you will know where to[7] go for specific information.

There are, however, mistakes that are caused by carelessness—mistakes you can[8] do something about immediately. See that names and addresses are spelled correctly. (No one likes to see his or[9] her name misspelled.) See that amounts of money mentioned in correspondence are correct. Suppose a dictator said,[10] "I am enclosing our check for $10 for four spools of wire at $2 a spool...." Something is wrong here. Four[11] spools of wire at $2 a spool would be $8. Or should the wire be $2.50 a spool,[12] which does come to $10? Check and double check.

Some letters are mailed even though the days and dates don't agree. For[13] example, the employer dictated, "I am looking forward to seeing you on Tuesday, June 9." In checking[14] your calendar, you find that Tuesday is June 8. Of course, something is wrong. Here is where you must speak to your employer.[15] You might say something like this: "I want to check on the day and date you are going to see the customer. Is[16] it Tuesday, June 8, or is it June 9, which is a Wednesday?"

Your employer may say to you, "If we don't hear from[17] Mr. Jones by June 15, let me know." Be sure you do just that. Put the information on your calendar pad—don't[18] trust it to memory.

Each day in the office is one of careful checking and double checking. You don't need[19] experience to do that—just interest in doing a good job. [393]

CHAPTER 10

LESSON 46

407 Dear Ms. Bennington: I will be moving to Los Angeles in three or four months, and I want to work for the city[1] government in some type of management position. I have been given your name by a mutual friend, Miss[2] Mary Harrington. She felt that you might be able to give me some ideas about which people to contact[3] to obtain a job with one of the city government agencies.

For many years I have been employed by the[4] state health department in Miami, and I have very good references. For the past year I have been working[5] in the accounting office under the direction of Mr. Lee Smith. I have been responsible for all major[6] financial reports for this department.

If you will let me know whom to see in Los Angeles, I will be[7] very grateful. Cordially yours,   [146]

409   Dear Mr. Dade: Because you are a member of the City Council, you are no doubt aware of the substandard[1] fire protection afforded the citizens of the southern section of our city. There are three fire stations in[2] the northern part of the town, but there is not a single fire station in my neighborhood.

Last week there was a[3] serious, frightening fire near my home, and it was fortunate indeed that the damage was kept as low as it was.[4] There could have been a great loss of life and property.

When you have an opportunity, won't you please help us get[5] prompt, efficient, and adequate fire protection, Mr. Dade. Yours very truly,   [114]

410   Dear Miss Bright: Thank you for writing about the possibility of the town's building a fire station in the[1] subdivision in which you live. I am certainly aware of the needs of this area.

You will be happy to[2] know that I am introducing a bill in the City Council on Friday, June 15, to build a fire station[3] on the southeast corner of the intersection of Fleet Avenue and First Street.

I will, of course, need the[4] well-organized backing of all residents of the area to get this bill through the council. You will be hearing more[5] from me later.

Thank you for your efforts to make our city a safer place in which to live. Sincerely yours,   [119]
78   Lesson 46

411   Dear Mr. Covington: Yesterday my life and property were in danger. As a member of the City Council,[1] you should be aware of an incident that occurred in the southern section of our city.

There was what appeared[2] to be a small grass fire which began in an area about 500 feet out of the city limits.[3] Trucks from the local fire station arrived at the scene quickly, but they did not attempt to extinguish the fire, which[4] was out of the city limits. After only a few minutes' time, the fire spread into the city and threatened[5] several homes, including mine. What could have been handled easily just a few minutes before suddenly became[6] a major problem.

It probably cost much more to extinguish the fire after it spread into the city[7] than it would have cost to smother it while it was confined to a small area outside the city limits.

Will[8] you please look into this matter soon; it is extremely urgent. Sincerely yours,   [174]

412   Dear Mr. Ray: Your very disturbing letter concerning the fire in your neighborhood was referred to me this[1] morning. Please be assured that I will look into this matter immediately.

I personally feel that the[2] action of the firefighters was reprehensible. I intend to do everything in my power to be[3] sure that such an incident does not occur again.

Thank you, Mr. Ray, for taking your time to report this[4] incident to me. Sincerely yours,   [86]

413   Dear Mr. Keith: I was quite disturbed to *read** in today's newspaper that the City Council is considering[1] closing the fire station at Third Street and Wilson Avenue. As you know, this is the only fire station in the[2] immediate area, and the residents of the neighborhood would not have adequate protection without this[3] station. Because this station was built only five years ago, I feel that closing it would be a waste of tax[4] money. If a station must be closed, a substitute should be chosen.

I understand that there is an effort being[5] made to build a new station in the southern part of the city, and I believe this is a *good*† idea.[6] However, I do not believe we should help one section of the city at the expense of another. Very truly[7] yours, [141]

Also correct:
*see
†fine, an excellent

LESSON 47

418 Dear Mr. Short: You will soon have an opportunity to let your voice be heard in Washington. On November[1] 6 you will be casting your vote for a senator from the state of Utah. As you know, our particular state[2] is not an ordinary one. Our people come from a wide variety of backgrounds, and they have a wide range[3] of interests. The people of our state need a senator who understands their needs and wishes. In my opinion,[4] I am the person they need.

For over 30 years I have been a resident of this state. I began working[5] in the order department of a large manufacturing company in Salt Lake City when I was 16[6] years old, and after a few months I ad-

vanced to the position of correspondence clerk. I was later chosen[7] to head the advertising department, a position I held for a period of five years. For the past[8] ten years I have been chief executive of the firm, which has more than doubled in size since I assumed control.

In[9] addition, I have had the advantage of being my district's representative in the city, county, and[10] state governments. I have won every election which I have entered. My record speaks for itself.

I am[11] relying on your vote, Mr. Short. Very sincerely yours, [231]

419 Gentlemen: Thank you for the support of your organization in helping to get an increase in the federal[1] appropriation for park development in the state of Hawaii. As a result of your efforts, the[2] federal government chose our state as a model for park development throughout the nation. Without your help,[3] I am sure that we could never have been as successful as we were.

As you know, the appropriation will be[4] increased from the current $1 million to $3 million. Although we had applied for $5 million,[5] I know that the amount set aside will give us an opportunity to develop several first-class[6] parks. We will be applying for another grant in a year or two; therefore, we will once again be asking[7] for your help. Sincerely yours, [145]

420 Dear Miss Gates: For the past several years the residents of the eastern part of Greenfield, Illinois, have become[1] increasingly concerned about the changing character of our neighborhood. When my family moved here ten years[2] ago, this area had no business whatever, and the residents were very proud of their quiet, well-maintained[3] neighborhood. But with the coming of business to the area, we have seen an increase in air pollution,[4] traffic, and litter.

We are not against business, of course, but we do want to maintain a clean, quiet[5] residential atmosphere in the neighborhood. We are sure you, too, are just as concerned about the quality[6] of life in our part of the city. Would it be possible for you, as mayor, to discuss this matter with a[7] group of residents of the area in the near future? We would like to present some ideas to you for[8] your approval. We would appreciate your replying to our request as soon as possible. Sincerely yours,[9] [180]

421 Dear Mr. Mason: The residents of the northern part of Boston, Massachusetts, have been conducting a clean-up[1] campaign during the month of April to help rid the area of litter. We are happy to report that[2] we have made considerable progress. We advertised in the local newspaper and distributed circulars[3] and other publications to all the homes in the area. In addition, we supplied 100 new[4] cement litter receptacles for use throughout the area. We are happy to report that there has been a[5] definite decrease in the amount of litter on the streets. Nearly all of the residents are complying[6] voluntarily with the rules we have set up. Best of all, we are experiencing a renewed sense of pride in[7] our community.

I would like to take this oppor-

tunity to suggest that you correspond with the residents[8] of other sections of our city and encourage them to engage in the same type of community-action[9] program. As mayor of the city, you are in a position to give public endorsement and publicity[10] to this type of program.

I am enclosing a folder which gives many ideas for public-improvement projects.[11] If you have any questions, I will be glad to answer them. Yours truly, [234]

422 Dear Miss Bennington: This is to acknowledge receipt of your report containing the information about the[1] neighborhood-improvement campaign you and your community have been conducting this summer in Boston, Massachusetts.[2] You are to be congratulated on the improvements you have made in the quality of life in the[3] area. In order to give your group proper recognition, we plan to publish your report in the local[4] newspaper next month.

The laudable example you have set is one that the entire city should follow, and I[5] will do everything possible to promote a city-wide campaign to improve the quality of life here next[6] year.

The city administration wishes to convey its best regards to you and your community, Miss Bennington.[7] Cordially yours, [144]

423 Dear Consumer: For the past few years the government has made a direct request to the people to *consume** less[1] energy. As you know, each year during the past decade energy consumption in this county has increased, but[2] the sources of energy have not been able to keep up with the demand.

We are *pleased*† to report that the people[3] have complied with our request. Energy consumption fell last year for the first time this decade, and we attribute[4] this decline to heightened awareness on the part of the public.

We want to offer our congratulations[5] to the general public on the good job that they have done and to appeal to our customers to keep up their[6] energy conservation program. Cordially yours, [130]

Also correct:
*use
†happy, glad

LESSON 48

427 Dear Mr. Black: It won't be long now. Many Americans are eagerly awaiting a "bonus" check from Uncle[1] Sam. Yes, that check will be an income tax refund.

If you get such a check, why not put it to work for you the[2] day it arrives. The Cleveland National Bank pays the highest interest the law allows.

Be frugal; when you receive[3] your refund, put it to work in a savings account at Cleveland National. Yours very truly, [78]

428 Dear Mr. Scott: It's that time of year again. In just a few weeks it will be time to file your income tax return[1] for the past year. If you are like most people, you will have a fairly large refund check, and the earlier you[2] send in your forms, the earlier you will receive that check.

If you have been putting off figuring your tax this year,[3] why not let the well-trained, experienced experts here at National Income Tax Service do the job for you.

Bring[4] in your records today and let us determine if you are eligible for a refund. Sincerely yours, [98]

429 To the Staff: As you have probably read, a new law has been passed which will have the effect of lowering the tax[1] of some employees for this year. In an effort to help you keep from having too much tax withheld each month, we are[2] asking you to fill out a new tax withholding form. This form will help you determine just how much tax you will owe[3] at the end of the year, and it will help the payroll department to deduct the proper amount.

Sometime this week,[4] please fill out, sign, and return the enclosed form to me. C. R. Jones [96]

430 Dear Miss Jones: Did you know that many American taxpayers will be receiving an income tax refund in[1] the next few months? Does this seem strange to you? It does to most people.

Employers are required by law to withhold a[2] certain percentage each pay period from their employees' checks. This exact amount is determined by the[3] employee.

Some people pay too little tax during the year and must remit a substantial amount at the end of[4] the year. However, some people purposely overpay their tax and receive a refund at the end of the year.[5] The effect is a kind of forced saving for them.

If the money had been put in a savings account, however, it[6] would have been drawing interest. If it is simply overpaid to the government, it draws no interest.

Why[7] not resolve to have only the exact amount you owe withheld each pay period and then open a savings[8] account in the First National Bank today. Cordially yours, [176]

431 Dear Miss Flint: If you are like many Americans, you will be receiving an income tax refund in a few[1] weeks. But if you are like some others, you will have to pay an additional amount because too little has been[2] withheld each pay period. To do so may easily deplete your financial reserves.

If you underestimated[3] your tax and find that you must make up the deficit this spring, you may need a loan. If you do, come to us.[4]

Because you have been a depositor in this bank for several years, you will not need to fill out any forms.[5] Just call us, and we will have your check waiting for you when you come in. Very truly yours, [116]

432 Dear Ms. Glass: As I am sure you are aware, the city will be facing a bond issue in the near future to[1] finance the construction of a new ball park. Some of the residents of our city would, of course, benefit by[2] the construction of such a park. But the *vast** majority would receive no direct benefit from it.

In[3] addition, residents of the city have been *asked*† to approve bond issues four times in the past two years. The Committee[4] for Responsible Government, which was organized last year to keep an eye on city taxes, would like to[5] call on you

to help us defeat this bond issue. Please vote no on Tuesday, February 15. Yours truly,[6]   [120]
Also correct:
*large
†requested

LESSON 49

436 Dear Mr. Little: During the months of January, February, and March the state ecology commission[1] will be checking pollution caused by the manufacturing plants along the banks of the Red River in Hudson[2] County. Your furniture manufacturing plant is one of those which we will be checking regularly during[3] this time.

We will be checking not only smoke emissions but also waste discharge into the river.

If you[4] wish further information concerning this project, call Miss Day, my secretary. Sincerely yours, [98]

437 Dear Mr. Little: As you know, for the past three months the state government has been checking the amount of pollution[1] caused by each of the manufacturing plants located along the banks of the Red River. I am happy[2] to say that your furniture plant easily met the standards which were set by the ecology commission.

Your[3] manufacturing plant caused less pollution than any other in the area, and I know that this is the[4] result of a great amount of time, energy, and work which you put into this effort.

May I congratulate[5] you on your success and encourage you to keep up the good work. Cordially yours, [114]

438 Dear Ms. Bennington: The Chamber of Commerce of Lexington is making a concerted effort to help the merchants[1] in the uptown business district obtain new parking facilities. As you know, several new shopping[2] centers have opened in the suburbs in the past few years, and business in the uptown area has decreased[3] steadily.

The members of the Chamber of Commerce cite several reasons for the area's decline, but[4] everyone believes that the main reason is the lack of satisfactory parking facilities. There is[5] one site which could readily be made into a parking area.

Enclosed is a map showing that site. When you[6] have had a chance to look over the enclosed material, please let me know if you are willing to join the other[7] merchants in the area in helping to revitalize our central business district. Sincerely yours,[8]   [160]

439 Dear Mr. Cunningham: Enclosed is a report prepared by the Board of Estimate giving the new tax valuation[1] which has been placed on your property at 1515 Elm Street. As you will note, the valuation has[2] been raised about 15 percent. This will mean that your tax on this property will be about 15 percent higher[3] than it has been during the past few years.

If you have any questions regarding the new valuation placed[4] on your property, please write me. Yours truly,   [88]

440 Dear Mrs. Wilson: In a study made of your property at 1416 Vine Street for the purpose of[1] setting a new tax valuation, we found two interesting things:

First, the property has not been reviewed[2] for 15 years. Second, a substantial addition has been made to the main house, but there is no record of this[3] addition on the tax records.

In light of these findings, we have raised the assessed valuation of your property[4] to $40,000, which we feel is fair. A complete, up-to-date report concerning your property is[5] enclosed. Yours very truly,   [105]

441 Dear Mr. Jones: Thank you for your letter explaining the new valuation placed on my property. I feel that[1] the new assessed valuation is reasonable. You are quite right; the last time the valuation was changed for[2] this property was about 15 years ago. However, please do not lose sight of the fact that we *obtained*★ a[3] city building permit before proceeding with the building.

Just to keep the record straight, I am enclosing a[4] *copy*† of this permit. If there is no record of this addition in your files, I am afraid the error was[5] made in your office. Very truly yours,   [107]

Also correct:
★got, received
†Xerox, photocopy

LESSON 50

444 Dear Mr. Strong: In today's newspaper I saw your notice about the political action committee you[1] plan to organize to help educate the voters of our state on controversial issues. I would like very[2] much to become a member of your group.

I have been away from the area for the past two years, but I returned[3] here in September and plan to make my permanent home in Westport. About ten years ago, a group similar[4] to yours was formed, and I was named chairman at that time. The group was disbanded, however, after only a[5] few months. Perhaps it was ahead of its time.

If I can do anything to help you with your organizational[6] meeting, let me know. Sincerely yours, [127]

445 Dear Dr. Rankin: Your welcome letter arrived in today's mail. Thank you for your offer to help with the next meeting[1] of the political action committee. As I am sure you are aware, our group is determined to be[2] a strong, positive force in the political life of our state, which is something that has been lacking up to this[3] time.

Three or four interested people are planning to have an organizational meeting on Friday,[4] November 10, at 8:30 p.m. in the Franklin Room of the State National Bank on Lexington Street. I hope[5] you will plan to be with us. Cordially yours, [108]

446 Dear Mr. Mendez: As you know, on November 5 you will have the opportunity to help shape the future[1] of our state. On that date you will go to the polls to help elect 20 new senators to four-year terms. Those new[2] senators will have the opportunity to change the course of events in the life of every man, woman,[3] and child in the state.

I hope you will take a few minutes of your time to read the enclosed folder telling about[4] my position on each of the major issues of the campaign. Then if you agree with my ideas, please plan to[5] vote for me

84 Lesson 50

for state senator on November 5.

When that date arrives, be sure your voice is heard in the state[6] capital. Get out and vote. Sincerely yours, [128]

447 Dear Mr. Gates: If you would like to see the property tax system in the state reformed, I hope you will consider[1] voting for me for state senator in the election in November.

For the past few years I have served as[2] mayor of the city of Midland, and I have become increasingly dissatisfied with the property tax[3] system of our state. I feel that by becoming a state senator, I will be in a very good position[4] to help restructure and reform this system.

Help update our tax system; vote for me in November. Revising[5] this system is long overdue, and I will lead the fight to do it. Sincerely yours, [116]

448 *Telephone Technique for the Secretary*

"Hello."

"May I ask who is speaking, please?"

"This is Kay Johnson."

"Is this Mr. Hoffman's office?"

"Yes, it is."

"May I[1] speak to him please? This is J. W. Jackson of the Arnold Products Corporation."

"Just a moment, I'll see[2] if he is in."

What is wrong with this telephone conversation? Only that it wastes about 20 words! What did[3] Kay Johnson, the new secretary, do wrong? Nothing serious. But if the phone had been answered, "Mr. Hoffman's[4] office," Mr. Jackson's time and patience would have been saved. Identifying the office is only one of the[5] important telephone techniques that the secretary should know.

Many new secretaries take telephone technique[6] for granted. "Oh, I've used the telephone ever since I was a child—there is nothing to it," is the typical[7] attitude toward learning good office telephone technique. But in an office, telephone technique can make friends[8] for your boss and your company, or it can lose them.

Knowing how to be effective on the telephone is[9] one of the secretary's greatest responsibilities. On the telephone the caller cannot see the person[10] who answers the phone, so the secretary's voice must convey personality, sincerity, and efficiency.[11]

The first rule of good telephone technique is to answer the telephone promptly. Never lose patience. Always[12] speak pleasantly and clearly; give your voice a tone that says, "I'm glad to help you, and I *can* help you."

Of course, being[13] pleasant and cheerful doesn't mean that you are eager to spend all day on the telephone. Your voice and your[14] efficient manner tell the caller that you are businesslike. But neither do you reveal that you are anxious to[15] get away as quickly as possible and with the least possible expenditure of energy.

Mind your manners[16] on the telephone! [324]

CHAPTER 11

LESSON 51

450 Dear Mr. Martin: Thank you for your inquiry of several days ago regarding a new-car loan from our[1] bank. You may, of course, complete all the paperwork by mail.

However, because you have not been a regular[2] depositor of ours, it will be necessary for you to fill out the usual credit application forms which[3] are enclosed.

As soon as we have been able to make a routine credit check which will take three or four days, we will[4] notify you so that you can place your order for the car you want. We are looking forward to doing business[5] with you. Cordially yours, [104]

452 Gentlemen: Enclosed are the forms which I completed in order to borrow money to purchase a new car. As[1] you will notice, I have included several credit references which I am sure you will find quite satisfactory.[2]

I hope you will be able to run the credit check quickly so that I may go ahead and purchase[3] a new car. I want to use the car on my vacation, which starts in two weeks; consequently, I would like to[4] complete all the paperwork by Monday, July 3.

I am looking forward to hearing from you shortly. Sincerely yours,[5] [100]

453 Dear Mr. Martin: We are sure that you will be happy to know that your credit has been approved up to a limit[1] of $6,000 for the purchase of a new car.

Now all you need do is shop around until you find[2] the car you want and then tell the automobile agency to get in touch with us. Our well-trained staff will handle[3] it from there.

We hope, Mr. Martin, that you will enjoy your new car and that it will serve you well for many[4] years. Yours very truly, [84]

454 Dear Friend: If you do not have the convenience of a safe deposit box for your valuables, it's time to act[1] now. Between now and February 12, you will be able to rent a safe deposit box for a full year for[2] half the regular price. Our offer is designed to introduce the safety and convenience of a First National[3] Bank safe deposit box to all our bank's regular customers.

When you have a safe deposit box, you will[4] no longer have to worry about keeping valuable papers at home. Fire cannot reach the interior[5] vault where the safe deposit boxes are located, and in the 50 years that the First National Bank has[6] offered this convenience to its customers, no thief has been able to reach the boxes either.

Give yourself total,[7] complete freedom from worry about fire, theft, and loss. Rent a safe deposit box at the First National Bank[8] today. Sincerely yours, [164]

455 Dear Mr. Thomas: When you decide to shop for a new car, stop first at the Eastern Savings Bank. In the time it[1] takes to drink a cup of coffee, you can fill out an application for an auto loan.

When you arrange a loan[2] with us, you will be dealing with a bank that makes twice as many auto loans as any other in this city.[3] We are ready to serve you. Cordially yours, [68]

456 Dear Mr. Baker: Your chances of enjoying a secure, comfortable retirement get better all the[1] time even if you work for an employer who doesn't have a pension plan. Here is why.

The government now allows[2] you to set up your own pension plan. You can create a personal retirement account and put into[3] it as much as 15 percent of your pay up to a limit of $1,500 a year.

We will be[4] glad to set up a retirement program for you at the Mutual Savings Bank. Stop in and let us give you[5] complete details. Very truly yours, [107]

457 Dear Depositor: If you do not already have a safe deposit box at the First National Bank, take[1] advantage of our special offer to our regular depositors. For a limited time our regular[2] depositors can rent any size box at half the advertised rate.

All you have to do is *stop** in at the bank, sign[3] a short form, and take possession of your box. When you *place*† your valuable papers in the box, no one will be[4] able to see them unless you want them to. In addition, they will be safe from fire and theft.

Come in today[5] and let us show you the best way to take care of your important papers. Yours very truly, [117]

Also correct:
*drop
†put

LESSON 52

462 Dear Mr. Kelley: Mr. James Hastings applied for a position with our bank yesterday and gave your name as[1] a reference. We understand that he worked for your publishing company in Indiana in the public[2] relations department for several years, but he left to take a position as a correspondent for[3] another business in Connecticut.

May we request that you fill out the attached reference sheet and return it[4] to us in the enclosed stamped, self-addressed envelope. We hope you will include any general comments you care[5] to make about Mr. Hastings. We would particularly like to have answers to the following questions:

1.[6] In what type of work do you feel he would be most successful?

2. Did he ever have difficulty in performing[7] his regular job responsibilities?

3. Was the general character of his work satisfactory?[8]

4. Were you satisfied with the quantity and quality of his work?

We hope to hear from you soon, Mr.[9] Kelley. Very truly yours, [186]

463   Dear Mrs. Overmeyer: I am very glad that Ms. Janice Perkins is being considered for a position[1] of responsibility with your organization. Ms. Perkins, who worked for our manufacturing[2] company in Delaware for two years, was no ordinary employee. She would usually arrive about an[3] hour early in the morning and depart well after closing time in the evening.

She made very rapid progress.[4] After she had been here only a few months, she was promoted from the order department to the advertising[5] department and received a substantial increase in salary.

Ms. Perkins took advantage of every opportunity[6] to be of service to the business and won the confidence and respect of all her peers. Management recognized[7] her potential immediately.

When Ms. Perkins left our company, she was being considered for a[8] very important job. We were sorry that she decided to leave this state. Sincerely yours,   [177]

464   Ladies and Gentlemen: Thank you for your inquiry concerning our hiring policies here at Eastern[1] Industries. We are glad to send you the information you requested.

We are an equal opportunity,[2] affirmative action employer. Our objective always is to employ the right person for the right job. All[3] positions which are open in our organization are advertised in the regular editions of[4] several newspapers throughout Maine, New Hampshire, and Vermont and are also printed in our company circular.[5] The applicants are given an opportunity to interview for the particular job they wish to obtain.[6] They are examined and questioned in those areas which are pertinent to their particular fields of interest.[7]

After the applicants are interviewed in the personnel department, usually three of them are referred[8] to the particular department where there is a job opening. Further interviews are conducted there. The[9] candidate best qualified for the job is hired immediately.

We hope that this information will be[10] helpful to you. Yours very truly,   [207]

465   Dear Mr. Mills: We are happy to acknowledge receipt of your letter requesting information about a[1] possible job in the correspondence department of the European Bank. Thank you, Mr. Mills, for your kind[2] remarks about our organization; we appreciate them.

At the present time we do not have a position[3] open in our finance section. Rather than hire outside people for the department, we usually promote[4] promising personnel from the company's accounting section. We do have two good jobs open in that section.[5] May I suggest that you consider beginning employment there.

If you would like to be considered for a[6] position as a full-time accountant, please fill out and return to us the enclosed application. Sincerely[7] yours,   [141]

466 Dear Mr. Short: Thank you for accepting our invitation to speak once again at the national convention[1] of the American Bankers Association on Tuesday, March 21. The subject of your speech, "Government[2] Control of Banking," certainly sounds intriguing.

We have always found your ideas interesting and your speeches[3] entertaining. We are looking forward to hearing you again this year. Very truly yours,   [77]

467 Dear Mr. Worth: Thank you very much for the time you took last week to interview me for the position as foreign[1] exchange specialist in your bank. Needless to say, I was impressed with your bank and its operation, Mr. Worth.[2]

I never realized that the bank was involved in so many varied, interesting areas of finance throughout[3] the world. The people who work in

your *organization** must be up to date on the latest financial[4] information concerning Europe, Asia, and Africa as well as our own nation. After visiting with you,[5] I am more convinced than ever that this is just the *field†* of work I would enjoy.

As we discussed, I will be[6] available to begin work next month if you decide to hire me. Cordially yours,   [135]
Also correct:
*company, business
†area, type

LESSON 53

471 Dear Mr. Jones: If you are planning a vacation this fall, take our advice: Don't carry a wallet full of cash;[1] take First National traveler's checks instead.

As you are well aware, losing your cash when you are away from home[2] is a very serious thing. When you carry First National traveler's checks, you will be able to replace[3] any checks that are lost or stolen very quickly. Just stop in at one of our branches which are located in[4] over 200 cities throughout the Southeast, and a courteous teller will replace your lost checks.

If you should[5] happen to be in an area where we do not have a branch, you will still be able to replace lost checks. We[6] have a check replacement arrangement with over 5,000 banks throughout the world.

Why not come in today, Mr.[7] Jones, and let us tell you all about the safety and convenience of First National traveler's checks. Sincerely[8] yours,   [161]

472 Dear Mr. Pace: I will be traveling to Europe, Asia, and Australia next summer, and it would be[1] advantageous for me to be able to cash checks at local banks during my trip if it should become necessary.[2] Would it be possible for you to give me a letter of introduction so that I could get ready cash if[3] the occasion should arise?

As your records will show, I have been a regular depositor of your bank for[4] a period of over 20 years. You have a complete list of my credit references. Please let me know as[5] soon as possible if your bank can issue me such a letter. Sincerely yours, [114]

473 Dear Mrs. Howard: Thank you very much for thinking of the Central National Bank when planning your vacation[1] for next summer. We will be happy to write a letter of introduction for you to use at banks in Europe, Asia,[2] and Australia.

As you may know, each individual bank may or may not honor such letters depending[3] on its own policies. However, we are happy to tell you that our bank has a fine working relationship[4] with hundreds of banks in various countries throughout the world.

Just drop by our bank any weekday between nine and[5] three, and we will be happy to have the letter signed by one of the bank's officers. Sincerely yours, [118]

474 Dear Ms. Miller: The General State Bank is now offering the highest interest rates allowed by law on its savings[1] accounts. For regular savings we have day-of-deposit, day-of-withdrawal accounts which pay 5 percent per annum[2] compounded quarterly. If money is left for as long as three months, it will draw 5½ percent interest.[3] For those who leave their money with us for six years, the interest rate can be as high as 7½ percent.[4]

Come in today, sign a simple form, and put your extra dollars to work for you. Your money will grow quickly.[5] Cordially yours, [103]

475 Dear Depositor: The General State Bank is your one-stop security shop. For many years we have offered[1] safe government-insured, high-interest-bearing accounts to to our depositors.

Since we opened our doors over 40[2] years ago, we have provided the maximum protection for our customers' valuable papers in[3] our fireproof safe deposit boxes.

Now we are proud to *announce** that beginning Wednesday, April 2, General[4] State Bank will sell American traveler's checks. As you probably know, these are the most widely used traveler's checks[5] in the country. In addition, they are *accepted*† in nearly every foreign country throughout the world.

Let the[6] General State Bank be your one-stop security shop. Come in today and begin taking advantage of the[7] General State Bank's safety features. Cordially yours, [149]
Also correct:
*say, tell you
†used

LESSON 54

479 Dear Miss Billings: It was very nice to see you again on my brief visit to Baltimore last May. I remember[1] fondly my seven years on the staff of your bank. It was a pleasure working in the various departments[2] there.

As you know, two years ago I moved to Chicago for personal reasons. Since that time I have not been working,[3] but I am planning to resume working here in the next month or two. I have applied for a position in[4] the credit department of the General State Bank, and I would like to use you as a reference. Will you please let[5] me know if I may do this. Please give my best wishes to the members of your staff. Sincerely yours, [117]

480 Dear Miss Perkins: Your visit to Maryland last month was a special treat for all of us. We were all very happy[1] to see you again. We would like very much to have you return to work here should you decide to live in the[2] Baltimore area once more.

I will, of course, be very happy to serve as a character reference for you.[3] Feel free to use my name on any personal data sheets which you submit when applying for a position.[4] Very truly yours, [84]

481 Dear Mr. Flynn: If you are interested in saving money on your life insurance when your present policy[1] expires, I am sure that the plans described in the enclosed four-page folder will be of special interest to[2] you.

The Central Savings Bank now offers life insurance to all its depositors at rates which are below those[3] of most of our major competitors. You will be able to insure all eligible members of your family[4] for one low monthly premium.

After you have had an opportunity to study the plans described in the[5] enclosed folder, won't you call me at 555-1701 and arrange for an appointment to discuss your[6] particular insurance needs. You will be making no mistake, Mr. Flynn, when you let the Central Savings Bank be[7] your exclusive agent for your life insurance needs. Sincerely yours, [153]

482 Dear Ms. Hastings: It is a pleasure on the occasion of your retirement to write you a letter of[1] congratulation on the many fine years of service you have given to the import and export division of[2] the Commercial State Bank of Wilmington.

Your contribution to the effectiveness and expansion of the[3] company's foreign market cannot be estimated in terms of money. You have helped to build company goodwill;[4] you have helped gain the confidence that thousands of our foreign customers have in us.

I know, Ms. Hastings, that you[5] will spend your time in many productive pursuits. When you visit Wilmington in the future, please stop in to see[6] us. You have our best wishes for a long, happy retirement. Sincerely yours, [134]

483 Dear Mr. Martin: It was a pleasure meeting James Green last week when you brought him to the office for an interview.[1] I am *happy** that he was impressed with the size and scope of our financial operations.

Yesterday I met[2] with Miss Frances Burke, who supervises the foreign exchange department. She suggested that despite Mr.[3] Green's fine financial background, we look a few more weeks to try to *locate*[†] a person who is better qualified[4] for the particular position we have open. She believes it would be a mistake to hire a person[5] without some experience in the field of foreign currency exchange.

I am, therefore, postponing making a[6] decision on the selection of a person until the first week of August. Cordially yours,   [137]
Also correct:
*glad, pleased
†find, get

LESSON 55

486 Dear Sir or Madam: I will be moving to Vermont in June to begin work at the eastern division offices[1] of International Industries, and I would like to open an account at your bank. Will you please let me[2] know if your bank has the feature of a credit-line account which I may use to make small loans by simply writing[3] checks. I am interested in having such an account with a credit line of at least $2,000.

Here[4] in Los Angeles the General State Bank, which previously handled my business, provided me with a regular[5] checking account, a savings account, a $2,000 line of credit, and a bank credit card. I[6] definitely would like to have these same conveniences at your bank. Yours very truly,   [135]

487 Dear Miss Temple: On Wednesday, July 15, the payroll procedure here at Standard Industries will be handled[1] on a new, entirely different basis. The First National Bank has devised a program whereby a major part[2] of our payroll work will be done by their staff.

The payroll procedure will be automatically simplified; it[3] will be completed without the issuance of a single check. Here is the way the new program will work: Before the[4] first of each month, we will send to the bank a list of the names of our employees and the amounts of their salaries[5] along with authorization to deduct the entire amount from our account. The bank will then deposit[6] each employee's salary directly to his or her individual account.

As an incentive for all[7] our employees to open accounts there, the First National Bank is offering free checking accounts to all[8] depositors who work at Standard Industries.

I genuinely hope that you will join us in this new venture, Miss[9] Temple. Sincerely yours ,   [184]

488 Dear Mr. Clay: As you probably know, your company, Standard Industries, has entered[1] into an agreement with our bank to help simplify its payroll procedures. Standard Industries will deposit[2] your payroll check directly to your account in our bank each pay period and will save you the time and effort[3] of coming to the bank personally. Your deposit will be made promptly on your regular payday, and you[4] will receive a deposit slip by mail verifying the transaction.

Because you already have an account[5] with our bank, the procedure authorizing us to handle your payroll deposit will be very simple. Just[6] sign and return the enclosed card, and we will begin crediting your salary directly to your account.[7] Incidentally, when you take part in this program, your checking account will be absolutely free of charge. Sincerely[8] yours,   [161]

489 *Pet Peeves About Office Workers*

Fifty employers were polled on their pet peeves about office workers. What they had to say will be of interest to[1] prospective office employees who want to avoid irritating the people under whom they will work.

Here is[2] a list of 11 of the pet peeves about office workers that are most frequently mentioned by employers:[3]

1. Office workers are slow to follow instructions or are unwilling to do so.

2. They flit from task to task[4] instead of organizing their work and completing one task at a time.

3. They ask questions every few minutes[5] instead of accumulating their questions and minimizing the number of interruptions necessary[6] to obtain answers.

4. Some workers ask no questions at all. Their mistakes, resulting from their failure to question[7] what is not clear to them, often mean that the work must be done over.

5. They receive too many personal[8] telephone calls in the office.

6. The attitude of many workers is that the world owes them a living.

7. They[9] waste too much time conversing with co-workers.

8. They are careless in their speech, often using slang expressions and[10] variations of yes and no.

9. They sometimes behave in a manner that is distracting and out of place in[11] an office.

10. They are often careless in proofreading and submit letters and other typewritten work with errors.[12]

11. They are absent too often.

It might be wise to review this list occasionally after you have obtained a[13] job just to be sure that you have not fallen into one or another of these careless and annoying behavior[14] patterns. Because such patterns are costly as well as irritating to employers, they may be responsible[15] for your failure to obtain a promotion.   [308]

CHAPTER 12

LESSON 56

491 Dear Friend: If you are interested in owning your own business, perhaps we will be able to make you an offer[1] that will enable you to be your own boss. National Printing Company, which was established almost 40[2] years ago, is now offering franchises in cities throughout the West to financially responsible[3] men and women who want to run their own businesses.

As you have probably heard on network television, the[4] National Printing Company is one of the most progressive franchise printing companies in the world. We have[5] more than 100 offices in 25 states, and we will be adding another 30 in the future.[6]

If you would like to have the wonderful feeling of being your own boss and yet be associated with one of[7] the country's leading business organizations, write to us as soon as possible and let us tell you how easy[8] it is to obtain a franchise. Sincerely yours,   [170]

493 Dear Miss Peters: Thank you for your letter of Saturday, August 18, requesting information about[1] acquiring a franchise from National Printing Company. Here is the information that you need in order to[2] make a decision.

1. The initial cost of a franchise is $10,000. When we receive this fee, we[3] will build your office and install for you the latest, most modern printing equipment.

2. During your first six months[4] of operation or until your gross sales reach $3,000 per month, you will pay no further fee to us.[5] After six months or when your sales reach that figure, you will begin to pay us 5 percent of your gross receipts each[6] month. This percentage will remain constant thereafter.

3. We will send a training representative to help you[7] with the operation of your business during the first month of operation. This representative will teach[8] you how to run your business.

4. We will run at least three general television commercials in your area[9] each month advertising the National Printing Company.

I hope, Miss Peters, that this information is[10] helpful to you and that you will soon become one of our franchise holders. If there is any other information[11] you wish, please write us again. We are looking forward to receiving your application. Sincerely, [238]

494 Dear Ms. Gordon: You will recall that three years ago I purchased a franchise from your company and have been[1] operating the business successfully since that time.

In my original contract I was assured that your[2] company would sell no other franchises within a 50-mile radius of my shop as long as I[3] operated it.

Last week I drove past the Central Shopping Center, which is about 20 miles from my shop. There I saw[4] a large sign which advertised that a new National franchise shop would be opening soon. As you can well understand,[5] I was very much upset by this. This is a clear violation of my contract, and I will protect my[6] rights in court if necessary.

I will expect to hear from you soon. Yours very truly, [136]

495 Dear Miss Mason: Your letter arrived in today's mail. I can understand your feeling concerning the protection[1] of your territorial rights with regard to your franchise with National Printing Company.

You will be[2] relieved to know that no other printing company will be operating in your area. What you saw was[3] indeed a National franchise sign, but it referred to another type of business which will not be in competition[4] with you in any way. It will, in fact, add to your business because National advertising will be[5] increased in your area as a result of the opening of this new shop.

If you have any further questions[6] about the new shop, please call me; I will be glad to answer them. Cordially yours, [134]

496 Dear Ms. James: Thank you very much for the help you gave me during the first six months while I was getting my new[1] business started here in Connecticut. It would have been impossible for me to have begun operation[2] alone. With your help I now feel that my franchise will become one of the most successful in the state.

You will be pleased[3] to know that October sales were up 5 percent over the preceding month. If the rate of sales during the first[4] ten days of this month continues, November will be even better.

Thanks to you and National Printing, I now[5] have a successful business in which I can be my own boss. Sincerely yours, [114]

497 Dear Mr. Wilmington: Thank you for filling our order for the printing of 70,000 copies of our[1] four-page circular that we will use to promote our new book, *The Advertisers Manual*. The circulars[2] arrived this morning, and we are very well pleased with them.

I have referred your bill for $800 to our[3] accounting department, and you should receive a check shortly.

Once again, Mr. Wilmington, thank you for your prompt[4] service. Doing business with you is a genuine pleasure. Sincerely yours, [93]

498 Dear Ms. Harper: Enclosed is a completed form in which I am applying for a franchise for a National[1] Printing Company shop. I understand that the initial fee will be $10,000 and that I will then[2] pay 5 percent of gross receipts thereafter. For these fees I am to *receive** a finished building, a complete set[3] of duplicating machines, the services of a consultant, and monthly advertising.

My partner and I[4] will be running the business on a full-time basis. Neither of us, however, has had experience in[5] operating office ma-

94 Lesson 57

chines or in *running*† a business of our own. Needless to say, we are going to need a[6] great deal of help.

Please let us hear from you as soon as you have had time to process our application. Sincerely[7] yours, [141]
Also correct:
*get, be given
†operating

LESSON 57

503 To All Employees: From time to time the management of the Nelson Corporation has issued special[1] memorandums to its employees in Texas, New Mexico, and Arizona concerning ethical practices.[2] The policies are simply an extension of the way in which we all live our personal lives, but we feel that[3] it is a good idea to restate them occasionally.

The policies cover such items as conflict[4] of interest, accepting gifts from suppliers, and personal use of company property. Please read carefully[5] the enclosed statement and then file it for future reference.

We all know that policy memorandums do[6] not of themselves create ethical business practices. It takes all of us working together and individually[7] to create the high standards which are characteristic of our business. James C. Lopez [158]

504 Dear Mr. Ward: It is a pleasure to answer your letter of Saturday, October 23. Our[1] organization, the Colorado Publishing Company, does indeed have a statement of guidelines for ethical[2] practices for all employees. I am enclosing a copy of these guidelines for your use.

You will note that while[3] no specific cases are covered, there are general statements concerning conflict of interest, political[4] contributions, and relationships with other businesses.

I hope, Mr. Ward, that you will find our guidelines[5] of help to you as you develop a set of your own for your organization. Sincerely yours, [118]

505 Dear Homeowner: If you are tired of living in a home that is old-fashioned because it was built a long time[1] ago, you may have thought about buying a new home in the suburbs. The new homes are certainly equipped with the[2] latest in modern conveniences and are beautiful to behold.

But think twice before you decide to buy that[3] new home. Check with the seller to determine exactly how much you will be paying for that convenience and[4] beauty. Perhaps you will still be paying for them long after you have become dissatisfied with them.

When you have had[5] a chance to think about this, come in to see us at the Florida Remodeling Company. For a fraction[6] of what you would ordinarily have to pay for a brand-new house, we can make your old home a beautiful,[7] convenient home. It can be the home of your dreams located in the same spot where you have lived over the years. You can[8] have all the modern conveniences without having to relocate your family, without having to find new[9] schools for your children, and without leaving your friends behind whom you would sorely miss.

And best of all, the cost of[10] re-modeling is far less than you might imagine. For an estimate of our low costs, call us today at[11] 555-1181. Cordially yours, [227]

506 Dear Mr. Gates: As you know, for the past three years you have been receiving the best electric service from the[1] Southern Electric Company in Mississippi. We are happy that we have been able to bring you[2] uninterrupted service at a price that is the lowest in the South.

During these past three years we have not increased our rates[3] to our customers although we have experienced a large increase in our own costs. At last month's meeting, the[4] City Council in Jackson doubled the taxes on our property on Park Street. Consequently, we must now raise our[5] rates; we have no other choice if we are to remain in business.

Beginning February 1, our rates will be[6] increased by 5 percent. We sincerely regret having to take this action, and we assure you that we will do[7] our best to hold the line on costs so that your electricity rates will not increase again in the near future.[8] Sincerely yours, [163]

507 Dear Mrs. Stacy: In this morning's mail I received my electric bill for the month of January, and I[1] was truly *surprised** to see that the amount of the bill was nearly double that of my December bill.

Because[2] I have been using approximately the same amount of electricity each month, I can see no reason[3] why there should be such an increase. I wonder, Mrs. Stacy, if there could be some mistake.

Several years ago[4] I *received†* a bill which contained an error caused by

Lesson 57   **95**

a misreading of my electric meter. Perhaps such a[5] misreading has occurred again this time. Will you please check to see if the bill is correct. Yours truly, [117]

Also correct:
*shocked
†got, was mailed

LESSON 58

511 Dear Miss Gold: A year ago the county began work on its new hospital located on Washington Avenue[1] between Fourth and Fifth Streets. We are pleased to announce that construction is progressing well. Unless unforeseen and[2] improbable circumstances arise, the hospital will open less than a year from now. It will provide the[3] citizens of our area with the finest, most up-to-date facilities in the state.

We are now beginning[4] to form our auxiliary organizations which will provide a valuable part of the services[5] offered by the hospital. One of the most important organizations will be the volunteer corps. We hope[6] to have 150 people who will visit the patients daily, deliver mail, and run the hospital[7] gift shop.

If you would like to join us and can give at least five hours' time a week, won't you call me for complete details.[8] Cordially yours, [162]

512 Dear Ms. Joyce: Thank you for the invitation to join the volunteer corps of the new county hospital. I feel[1] that the work you and your group will be doing is extremely important and will help the hospital immeasurably.[2] Countless people throughout the entire area will benefit from your work. I am

happy to accept[3] your invitation, and I know I will enjoy our association.

For the next few weeks, however, I will[4] be away from the city on vacation. Therefore, it will be impossible for me to take part in the[5] organizational work of the group.

When I return from my vacation, which will be about September 2 or[6] 3, I will write you. Sincerely yours, [127]

513 Dear Miss West: We are happy that you will be working as a member of our hospital volunteer corps beginning[1] in September. I know that you, in your role of hospital volunteer, will make a real contribution to[2] the success of our organization.

Enclosed is an application form which I would like you to complete and[3] return to us at your convenience. This will help us keep accurate records on all our volunteers.

You will be[4] glad to know that we now have over 100 volunteers on the rolls, and our goal of 150[5] volunteers will probably be reached in the next week or two.

Welcome to our organization, Miss West. We know you[6] will enjoy serving your community in this fine way. Yours very truly, [134]

514 Dear Mr. Casey: Thank you for your generous contribution to our hospital fund. I am happy to[1] report that contributions have been coming in steadily since June 15, and I am confident that we will reach[2] our goal of $900,000, which is the amount we estimate the new hospital wing will cost.

A[3] receipt for your contribution is enclosed. Sincerely yours, [71]

515 Dear Dr. Taylor: If the past few years can be used to predict the future, this fall the residents of the East[1] Coast can expect an unpleasant flu epidemic. As you know, last year the *residents** of the entire area[2] suffered the worst flu epidemic in the past quarter century. The East Coast Medical Society[3] is making an all-out drive this year to reduce the number and severity of cases of flu.

On Monday,[4] September 12, there will be a public radio, television, and newspaper *campaign†* to encourage[5] everyone to get shots before the flu season begins. We hope to enlist the assistance of every[6] physician on the East Coast. May we depend on you to help in this program, Dr. Taylor? Please read the enclosed[7] booklet and then call our office for further information. Sincerely yours,   [153]

Also correct:

*people, citizens

†advertisement, message

LESSON 59

519 Dear Miss Macy: Recently I visited a friend who lives just a few miles from my home here in Weston. In her home[1] she has excellent television reception from the four local channels and also from three other channels[2] because she is a cable television subscriber.

When I returned to my home, I called the cable[3] television company and asked if I could subscribe to this service. I was surprised to learn that while the company[4] has the right to operate throughout the city of Jackson, they cannot operate here in Weston because[5] of a city regulation. I cannot understand why we should suffer such a penalty simply because we[6] choose to live in Weston rather than in Jackson. I hope, Miss Macy, that you will use your influence with the[7] City Council to help get this service for our city as soon as possible. Very truly yours,   [158]

520 Dear Dr. Bates: We chose your name at random from the local telephone book, and we would like you to participate[1] in a television survey the week of December 3. Our company, the Texas Television Rating[2] Service, is one of the oldest, most respected television rating companies in the country. We have[3] been conducting rating surveys in every area of the United States for over 20 years, and[4] we are proud of our record of dependability and reliability.

If you choose to participate[5] in the survey, we will send you a log in which you will keep an exact record of the time you view television[6] for a complete week. You would be one of several thousand people we chose to represent the American[7] public.

We do not pay the participants in the survey, but we do give them the opportunity[8] to take part in a meaningful way in helping to shape the future of television broadcasting. Your vote for[9] a particular program will help the producers of that show keep it on the air.

Please let us know if you would[10] like to participate in this survey. Cordially yours,   [210]

521 Dear Mr. Pace: I will be happy to participate in your company's television survey which will be[1] conducted the week of December 3. I feel it will be an interesting experience to take part in[2] such a survey.

Please send me all the materials I will need to keep a record of my viewing time along[3] with complete instructions. I look forward to hearing from you. Very truly yours, [74]

522 Dear Dr. Peters: Thank you very much for agreeing to participate in the television survey which[1] our company, the Texas Television Rating Service, will be conducting in your area the week of[2] December 3. Enclosed are two logs for you to use during this week—one for each of the two television sets[3] in your home.

As you will note, the time for each of the seven days in the week has been apportioned into 15-minute[4] intervals. Please keep each log by the television set. When you watch a particular show, be sure to[5] note that in the log immediately. If you watch for 5 minutes or more in any 15-minute[6] period, please make a note of this. Do not bother to note any viewing of less than 5 minutes.

If you have any[7] questions about the survey, please call me at (800) 555-3587, which is our toll-free number.[8] At the end of the week, just sign the two logs, place them in the self-addressed envelope, and return them to me.[9]

Thank you very much, Dr. Peters, for your participation. We are grateful for your cooperation. Sincerely[10] yours, [201]

523 Dear Mr. Davis: As you know, since April 15 we have been sponsoring a 15-minute program on[1] television station WQAT advertising our clothing. Because of budgetary considerations,[2] we will have to discontinue this program when our present contract expires on July 18.

We[3] regret having to take this action, Mr. Davis, but we have no alternative because of business conditions[4] in our industry. Sincerely yours, [87]

524 Dear Mr. Kelley: After waiting more than a week to get your television set repaired and then having your[1] appointment canceled, you have every right to demand a refund for the amount you paid for your service[2] policy.

There can never be a good excuse for the poor service you received from our *company*,* but I would like[3] to tell you the reason. The week of July 4 is always a difficult one for any type of service[4] company. We try to schedule vacations for our employees so that they do not come on this weekend, but we always[5] seem to have a few employees who need this time off. This year we had three technicians on vacation for the[6] entire week. To make matters worse, our service manager was at home ill with the flu. I am afraid our past record[7] of dependability, reliability, and efficiency slipped considerably during this[8] time.

What we want to do now is to regain your confidence. If you will give us just one more chance, I will *come*† to[9] your home personally at your convenience and guarantee to get your set in top working order. Just call[10] me at 555-7879; I will be waiting to hear from you. Yours very truly, [217]

Also correct:
*organization, business
†drive

LESSON 60

527 Dear Miss Newton: We at the Denver Department Store are delighted that you can be with us for the entire week[1] of February 4. We have made arrangements for you to stay at the Freedom Hotel, which is located at[2] 15 Broadway. A member of our department, Mr. Charles Norton, will meet you at the air terminal if you[3] will tell us which plane you are taking.

Needless to say, we plan to place an advertisement in the *Daily Bulletin*,[4] our local newspaper, to inform the public that you will be available for consultations on[5] flower arranging during the week. Sincerely yours, [109]

528 Dear Customer: During the week of February 4, Miss Janet Newton will be in our Denver store to[1] demonstrate the art of flower arranging for our customers. We hope you will plan to attend at least one of the[2] demonstrations.

Miss Newton is a well-known, internationally recognized authority on floral[3] arrangements and is in great demand for personal appearances. Between the hours of nine and five each day during[4] the week, our customers will have the opportunity to watch Miss Newton, to ask her advice on their own[5] decorating problems, or to have her create a special, one-of-a-kind flower arrangement for them.

We look[6] forward to having Miss Newton in Denver, and we hope you will take advantage of this special opportunity[7] to meet one of the nation's most prominent floral designers. Very truly yours, [155]

529 Dear Mr. Brown: The week I spent in Denver, Colorado, working with your excellent staff and demonstrating[1] the art of floral design for your customers was a real pleasure for me. Thank you for making this week such an[2] enjoyable experience.

I hope that as a result of my visit, you will ultimately establish[3] a permanent flower department in your store. As you know, my company has a complete line of fine[4] artificial flowers. If we can be of service to you, please let us know. Yours very truly, [96]

530 Dear Miss Newton: Your visit to Denver was a big success! Thank you very much for taking time from your busy[1] schedule to spend a week with us.

When you left, many of our customers told us how impressed they were with your[2] ability and your willingness to share your decorating ideas.

As a result of your visit, many[3] of our customers have inquired about your line of artificial flowers, and I have decided to add a[4] permanent flower department, which will take the place of the flower section in our gift shop. We will, of course, be[5] ordering flowers from your company.

Thank you again, Miss Newton, for the wonderful week. Sincerely yours, [118]

531 *Good Work Habits Win Promotion*
Frank Jones had a good job waiting for him the day he finished school. He was employed in the freight offices of a[1] large railroad company. Frank was hired as a stenographer for three executives. He

took their dictation, typed[2] reports, and made himself useful in every way he could. He was a hard worker, and he enjoyed the challenge[3] of keeping three executives equally happy. And they were pleased with his performance.

Frank soon noticed that some[4] of the other young people who began their employment there at the same time he did were not so diligent. One[5] of them regularly arrived ten or fifteen minutes past the starting hour in the morning. Another frequently[6] took more than the time allowed for lunch. Still another always left early at the end of the day. As far[7] as their work was concerned, they seemed interested only in getting by.

Frank began to wonder. "I work hard," he[8] thought. "I follow all the rules and try to make every minute count. These people disregard the rules and don't seem[9] to turn out nearly as much work as I. Yet they get the same salary that I do. Who is right—they or I?" But[10] in spite of his confusion, Frank continued to do his best.

After nine months Mr. Hanson, the general freight[11] agent, called Frank into his office and told him about the fine reports he had received about Frank's work. Because[12] of his excellent record and his ability to accept responsibility, Frank was being promoted[13] to the position of executive assistant to the general freight agent.

Of course, this was an[14] important promotion for Frank. He had won it by hard work and by taking his responsibilities seriously.[15] Those who didn't stick by the rules or didn't care very much about the quantity and quality of their[16] work were left standing still. Frank was on his way up.   [329]

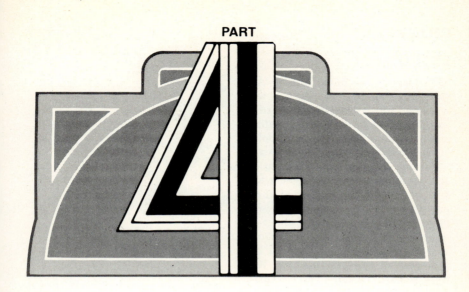

PART

Chapters 13-16
Lessons 61-80

CHAPTER 13

LESSON 61

533 Dear Miss Buckingham: As you know, on Saturday, July 4, we will be celebrating the nation's birthday. The[1] city of Austin is planning many major events which should attract visitors from the entire area.[2]

At our meeting several months ago we decided on the people who will be in charge of each of the[3] major activities except the children's programs. At our meeting about a week ago the members of our[4] committee thought that you would be the ideal person for this job. We hope you will be able to accept this[5] responsibility.

We feel we should have at least three or four activities for the children, but definite plans have[6] not yet been made. I hope you will let me hear from you as soon as possible. Sincerely yours, [137]

Office-Style Dictation

534 *(As dictated)* Dear Friends: As you probably know, this year marks our city's one-hundredth anniversary. To help in the celebration of this (after *help*, make that *celebrate this*) event (no, *occasion*), on Friday, Saturday, and Sunday, July 2, 3, and 4, the historic ship (make that *steamship*) "River Queen" will be at the Fifth Street dock. There will be many (no, *several*) exhibits on the steamship designed to reflect life as it was during the time (make that *at the time*) of the city's birth 100 years ago. At the time the steamship is in the Fifth Street berth, there will be delightful (no, *special*) programs and entertainment in the...

534 *(As it would be transcribed)* Dear Friends: As you probably know, this year marks our city's one-hundredth anniversary. To help celebrate this[1] occasion, on Friday, Saturday, and Sunday, July 2, 3, and 4, the historic steamship "River Queen" will[2] be at the Fifth Street dock. There will be several exhibits on the steamship designed to reflect life as it was[3] at the time of the city's birth 100 years ago. At the time the steamship is in the Fifth Street berth, there will[4] be special programs and entertainment in the... [89]

536 Dear Mr. Billings: It is a pleasure indeed to accept your invitation to direct the children's[1] activities at the July 4 celebration in Austin. I will assume my duties just as soon as I return[2] from my vacation, which will be early in May.

In the meantime, I have several questions which I hope you will[3] be able to answer for me.

1. Will I have a special budget? If the answer is yes, how much will I have[4] to spend?

2. Where will the children's events be held?

3. Should the boys' and girls' contests be held separately, or would[5] you like to have combined events?

When you have a few moments, please answer these questions for me. Sincerely yours, [119]

537 Dear Friends: As you probably know, this year marks our city's one hundredth anniversary. To help celebrate this[1] occasion, on Friday, Saturday, and Sunday, July 2, 3, and 4, the historic steamship "River Queen" will[2] be at the Fifth Street dock.

There will be several exhibits on

the steamship designed to reflect life as it was[3] at the time of the city's birth 100 years ago. At the time the steamship is in the Fifth Street berth, there will[4] be special programs and entertainment in the immediate vicinity and in the adjacent neighborhoods.[5] We are expecting over 20,000 visitors during the three-day period that the steamship will[6] be in our city.

"River Queen" is the state's only historic exhibit on tour this year, and we know that you[7] and your children will want to take a guided tour through it. Yours very truly, [154]

538 Dear Friends: The visit of the historic steamship "River Queen" to our city on July 2, 3, and 4 was a[1] great success. Thank you for helping to publicize this event. You will be pleased to know that over 25,000[2] people visited "River Queen" while it was berthed at the Fifth Street dock.

Because it was such a big,[3] unprecedented success, there will definitely be a similar event next year. If you have any suggestions as[4] to ways in which we can make next year's event even more successful, please send them to me; they will be gratefully[5] received. Sincerely yours, [104]

539 Dear Mr. Jones: One winter 33 years ago the people in Phoenix saw snow. It was one of those rare[1] winter days when it was too nippy for swimming and golfers had to put on a sweater. However, we are spoiled here[2] in Phoenix. When it is nasty in the East, we are basking under the warmest skies in the United States.

Take[3] December, for example. You can expect every day to be sunny and balmy.

Why not plan to come to[4] Phoenix for your vacation this coming winter. You will have a vacation that you will long remember.

To learn[5] about all the things Phoenix has to offer vacationers, send for a copy of our booklet, *Phoenix in the[6] Winter*. We will be delighted to send it to you. Sincerely yours, [133]

540 Dear Mr. Case: I read in the Friday, June 15, newspaper that the state government is planning to send a[1] historic steamship to Houston to help celebrate the city's birthday.

I would like to take my children to see[2] the many displays which will be aboard the ship. Will you please let me know when the ship will be here, which berth will be[3] used, and the times that the *ship** will be open to visitors. I would also like to know if there will be a fee[4] charged for admission and if there will be a special lot set aside where visitors may *park*† their cars.

We are all[5] looking forward to seeing this great old steamship, Mr. Case. Cordially yours, [114]
Also correct:
*steamship, boat
†leave

LESSON 62

545 Dear Dr. Childs: In yesterday morning's newspaper there was an article regarding the possible construction[1] of an amusement park in Greenville. I am a resident of this suburban area, and I would like[2] to register my objection to the construction of this park.

The newspaper stated that if the park was built,[3] there would ordinarily be a minimum of 20,000 people there every day and that they would[4] arrive in more than 5,000 cars. The addition of this extra traffic to the streets of this neighborhood, which[5] are usually very crowded to begin with, would create a very difficult, aggravating burden[6] for the residents of this area.

I hope that you, as president of the City Council, will do[7] everything you can to prevent the construction of this park. Very truly yours, [154]

546 Dear Ms. Casey: Please pardon my slight delay in answering your letter concerning the construction of the[1] amusement park which has been proposed for Greenville. We are happy to receive letters about community affairs[2] from interested citizens.

The members of the City Council certainly understand the problems which could[3] be created by the addition of more than 5,000 cars to the present streets in the area of the[4] proposed amusement park. We want to assure you, Ms. Casey, that we will never permit a park of the magnitude[5] described in the newspaper to be built without first being sure that the traffic problems would be solved long[6] before the scheduled opening of the park. Thank you for your interest. Sincerely yours, [135]

547 Dear Mr. Keith: Thank you for your request for information about the reasons why the City Council is[1] considering approving the new

amusement park in Greenville.

As you know, the past year has not been a[2] particularly good one for the people of our city. The unemployment rate has gone up 2 percent, and a major[3] manufacturing plant has moved away from the area.

These are the main reasons why the members of the[4] City Council are reluctant to discourage any business which wishes to locate here. If the council does[5] approve the park, I can assure you that it will be a first-class attraction and that every step will be taken[6] to prevent the park from becoming a nuisance to the neighborhood's residents.

Our main purpose is to make[7] Greenville an even better place in which to live. Very truly yours, [152]

548 Dear Mr. Collins: It was indeed a pleasure to read in the newspaper that a national company is[1] planning to build a new shopping center in Minneapolis, Minnesota, next year. If this shopping center[2] is built, I know it will bring a great deal of business to our area.

I am aware, of course, of the prevailing[3] attitude that such a center would increase traffic and disrupt the lives of the local residents. However,[4] I want to encourage the City Council to approve this project. If it is approved, it will provide jobs,[5] money, and convenience for the many residents of our community. Sincerely yours,   [117]

549 Dear Mr. Smith: I would like to take this opportunity to protest the proposed construction of the new[1] manufacturing plant in metropolitan Omaha. As you know, the plant is proposed for a site near the[2] football stadium.

I am sure you are aware of the problems in our area during the fall months when teams from[3] all over Nebraska are using the stadium. It is almost impossible for those who live near the[4] stadium to drive down the streets, and the parking spaces in front of our homes are often occupied by the cars of[5] football fans. The construction of a new manufacturing plant in the area would mean that the problem would[6] be intensified.

Because a number of my friends in this area feel as I do, we are forming a[7] committee of interested persons to attempt to convince the City Council to abandon the idea.[8] Our first meeting will be next Thursday, August 13, at my home at 8 p.m. When we meet, we would be happy[9] to have you speak to us; your comments will be welcome. Very truly yours,   [193]

550 Dear Mr. Childs: Thanks for taking time to respond to my recent letter concerning the amusement park which is[1] proposed for our city. I'm afraid, however, that I did not find your letter to be reassuring. Despite[2] your feelings concerning the desirability of *putting**** such a park in our city, I firmly believe[3] that it will be nothing but a problem for the majority of the residents of the area.

Believe[4] me, Mr. Childs, I am aware of the economic problems faced by this *part*† of the city during the past[5] year. I would like just as much as anyone to reduce the unemployment rate and to get more business in our[6] area. But let us try to

get businesses which will not disrupt the lives of the city residents. Yours[7] very truly,   [142]
Also correct:
****erecting, establishing
†section, area

LESSON 63

554 Dear Ms. Day: Thank you for your interest in the new musical comedy we plan to produce for the fall[1] theater season. If all goes well, we plan to take the show on a tour of the principal cities throughout the United[2] States for a three-month period prior to its Broadway premier next year. We are quite excited about the[3] show, and we believe that it will be well received by the general public.

We are, of course, looking for financial[4] backers for the show. We will be having a dinner meeting for potential backers at the Lexington Inn[5] on Monday, January 21, at 8 p.m. We will attempt to raise at least $200,000[6] at that time. If you would like to attend, just let us know and we will reserve a place for you. Cordially yours,[7]   [140]

555 Dear Miss Dutton: Please reserve a place for me at the dinner meeting for potential backers of the new musical[1] comedy which your organization is sponsoring on Monday, January 21. I am[2] especially interested in investing because I believe that this show has a very good chance of being[3] financially successful.

I am looking forward to meeting you socially, Miss Dutton. Sincerely yours,   [79]

556 Dear Mr. Sample: On Tuesday, March 14, the people of Arkansas will go to the polls to vote on a[1] proposal which could authorize issuance of over $15 million in bonds to improve the parks in the[2] state.

As you know, Arkansas, which has many fine, well-kept parks, needs several more to meet the needs of the people.[3] Approximately half the money would go to improve the existing parks while the other half would be used to[4] purchase land for future development.

I hope you will take time to vote for this issue; it will make Arkansas[5] an even better state in which to live. Very truly yours,   [111]

557 Dear Mrs. James: On Wednesday, April 2, you will have an opportunity to help improve the quality[1] of life in Washington County. That is the date on which you will be asked to approve a county park bond issue.[2]

As you probably know, we simply do not have ample park facilities for our citizens' needs. During the[3] summers the seven county parks are overcrowded and the facilities are inadequate. Each weekend[4] excess traffic must be turned away from each of the parks.

Here are the facts for your consideration: North Park now has[5] three tennis courts; it should have at least ten. South Park has no swimming pool; consequently, the residents in that[6] area must travel ten miles to have access to a public pool. A new pool is highly desirable. Central[7] Park badly needs major renovation. The other four parks are much too small and should be expanded. In addition,[8] new parks are

needed in the eastern, western, and central parts of the county.

But all this costs money. When you[9] go to the polls on April 2, won't you please vote for the parks bond issue. The people of our county deserve good[10] parks. Your vote can help the people get them. Cordially yours,   [210]

558 Dear Mr. James: We were happy to have your letter of February 15 requesting information[1] about the Western Ranch. The enclosed brochure contains pictures of our facilities and describes the recreational[2] opportunities that are available to you and your family.

We think you will particularly[3] enjoy riding on our 50 miles of beautiful trails. Hundreds of people from all over the United States[4] come here to take advantage of our riding facilities.

Our rates are listed on page 18 of the brochure,[5] and on page 19 there is a reservation form.

We hope, Mr. James, that we will see you on your vacation[6] this year. Sincerely yours,   [124]

559 Dear Mrs. Gates: When a family has a Nelson swimming pool in its yard, you can be sure it is a happy[1] family. That is where everyone gets his or her exercise in the summer and where everyone's friends[2] are entertained.

A Nelson pool is produced and installed by the most respected pool builder in the world. We have[3] been building swimming pools for more than 40 years.

We will be glad to tell you how easy it is to install a[4] Nelson pool if you will return the enclosed card. Sincerely yours, [92]

560 Dear Ms. Harrington: For the past ten years the Smith County Chamber of Commerce has been attempting to get the[1] *voters** of the county to approve a bond issue to improve the local parks. We have attempted to get the[2] issue passed on two separate occasions. Unfortunately, it was defeated both times.

We need to act now to[3] preserve the vast open area left in the county for future park use. On Thursday, May 7, the voters[4] will again have the opportunity to vote for expanding and improving the seven parks in the county.[5] We hope that you, as state senator from this county, will recommend the *approval†* of this bond issue. Your[6] endorsement could mean the difference between success and failure. Yours very truly,
[134]

Also correct:
*people
†passage

LESSON 64

564 Dear Mr. Torres: Once again this summer the Alabama Drama Association will feature a[1] three-month appearance of the American Repertory Theater. We are offering a book of 20 tickets[2] good for any of the performances of the four plays to be presented. The tickets may be used for one[3] performance, or they may be used in any combination during the months of June, July, and August.

These tickets[4] will provide an evening of fine entertainment for you and your family. In addition, they will make[5] perfect gifts for out-of-

state visitors. When you have a book of tickets, all you need do is call us a few days[6] before the particular performance you wish to see, and we will reserve seats for you.

But best of all, Mr.[7] Torres, you will have the good feeling that you are helping to sponsor one of the state's most worthwhile cultural[8] activities, and you will be helping to assure its continued success in the future. Incidentally, if you[9] enter your order for tickets before Sunday, May 1, you will receive a special 25 percent discount.[10] Sincerely, [202]

565 Dear Mr. Torres: Enclosed are the tickets to the American Repertory Theater. Thank you for supporting[1] this worthwhile project.

As you know, there are four plays which will be running during the months of June, July, and August.[2] You may use your tickets all for one performance, or you may use them in any combination you wish. To[3] obtain the actual tickets for a specific performance, just call the box office a few days prior to the[4] show you wish to see, and we will reserve the best seats available for you.

Incidentally, you are entitled[5] to a free tour of our facilities whenever you are in the neighborhood. The Park Avenue entrance to[6] the theater is open from 10 a.m. until 4 p.m. Monday through Friday. Simply walk in; no appointment[7] is necessary.

Best wishes for a delightful, entertaining summer. Sincerely yours,
[157]

566 Dear Mr. Green: During the week of September 4, I will be on vacation in Los Angeles. While I am[1] in the neighborhood of Burbank, California, I would like to attend several television programs. Will[2] you please check the taping schedule and send me two tickets each for any shows which will be taped on September 4,[3] 5, and 6.

I am a student studying radio and television advertising at Western State[4] College here in Alaska, and I would appreciate having a tour of your television studios in Los[5] Angeles if you can arrange it. Please let me hear from you as soon as possible. Very sincerely yours,   [119]

567   Dear Mr. White: Thank you for thinking of our television network when you planned your trip to our neighborhood. I[1] am happy to tell you that there will be three programs taped during the time you will be in Los Angeles. Enclosed[2] are two tickets for each of the three programs.

In addition, we have two regular daily tours of our studio[3] facilities. The morning tour, which leaves the main building at ten, costs $2 per person. You may obtain[4] your tickets at the studio on the day you wish to see the facilities.

I hope you have a very pleasant[5] visit to California, Mr. White. Very cordially yours,   [113]

568   Dear Mary: I am sending you today by express a copy of a new book just published by the Nelson[1] Publishing Company called *Tennis Anyone!*

As you know, tennis has been my favorite sport ever since I was[2] a child, and I have always considered myself a good player. I bought a copy of *Tennis Anyone!*[3] because I was

intrigued by the title and not because I thought it would teach me anything.

However, I was[4] delighted with the many practical suggestions I found that I know will improve my game substantially.

After[5] you have read *Tennis Anyone!* I guarantee you will be a better tennis player. Sincerely,   [118]

569   Dear Mr. Best: Two weeks ago Jim Brown showed his film on platform tennis to about 150 platform[1] tennis enthusiasts who were able to squeeze their way into our store. After the showing of the film, he[2] answered questions for almost an hour. We are sorry that you could not attend because we know you would have enjoyed[3] meeting Jim and profited from the showing of his film and listening to his comments.

May we remind you, Mr.[4] Best, that we have a complete line of platform tennis equipment. Come in soon and stock up for the season that is[5] about to begin. Sincerely yours,   [107]

570   Dear Miss Simms: When I was on vacation in Philadelphia last year, I found myself in the neighborhood of[1] your television network affiliate there. I stopped in just at the right moment, and I was able to[2] *attend** the taping of an audience-participation show. Needless to say, I enjoyed it very much. This year[3] I will be in New York on vacation, and I would like to be a contestant on one of your future shows if[4] this is possible.

I understand that you usually interview *contestants†* before they appear on your[5] programs. Will you please schedule such an interview for me. I will be in New York for the entire month of October.[6] Thanks for your consideration. Yours truly, [129]

Also correct:
*see, view
†people, persons

LESSON 65

573 Dear Miss Gardner: As you know, the third annual Brown County Fair will be held at City Coliseum on[1] Friday, Saturday, and Sunday, September 1, 2, and 3.

I have been named director of this year's fair, and I am[2] now planning a number of special events which I hope will be popular with the visitors. If you would like[3] to recommend that any special events be included in this fair, please let me know as soon as possible.[4] I would like to have your suggestions. Cordially yours, [90]

574 Dear Mr. Trenton: Thank you for requesting my recommendations about the type of events we should have at[1] the third annual Brown County Fair. I am happy to pass along a few ideas, Mr. Trenton.

While I[2] do not now have any specific suggestions to make, I feel that a county fair should include events of wide[3] appeal to men, women, and children of every age group. We should have attractions for everyone from small[4] children to senior citizens.

If I can be of help to you as you plan the fair, please let me know. Sincerely[5] yours, [101]

575 Dear Mrs. Jack: I just read in today's newspaper that Brown County is planning to have a fair on September[1] 1, 2, and 3 this year. Frankly, I am delighted that the fair will be held again this year; my family and[2] I particularly enjoyed last year's program. The special events held in the arena were outstanding, and[3] we enjoyed them immensely.

Would you please send me complete, detailed information about the fair including the[4] price of admission, the special events which are planned, and the hours the fair will be open. In addition, I would[5] like to know the cab fare between the train station and the fairgrounds. I look forward to receiving your reply.[6] Sincerely yours, [123]

576 Dear Mr. Lexington: Thank you for your inquiry about the plans for the Brown County Fair. When our advertising[1] brochure is ready, I will see that you receive a copy.

There will be no admission fee at the gate, and most[2] of the special exhibits will be free. There will be a small admission charge for the children's rides, the talent show,[3] and the baseball game. Admittance to the opening night banquet, which will be held in the Hotel Baker, is by[4] invitation only.

We have hired a bus to run between the train station and the coliseum during the[5] three days of the fair. A special round-trip bus fare of $2 will be charged; you may purchase your bus ticket at[6] the station.

I hope you will enjoy the fair as much as we are enjoying planning it. See you at the fair![7] Cordially yours, [142]

577 Dear Miss Lee: I read in yesterday's *Times* that your organization, the Texas Fine Arts Club, will again sponsor[1] the Art Fiesta in San Antonio each weekend in April. I recently moved to Texas, and I would[2] like to exhibit some of my paintings at the fiesta this year.

Will you please let me know all the details so[3] that I can make arrangements to have a representative sample of my work on display.

May I congratulate[4] you and your organization for the fine work you are doing. Sincerely yours,   [95]

578   Dear Ms. Barnes: If you have always wanted to spend a vacation on the beautiful island of Bermuda, now[1] is the time to do so. Beginning September 15, our special low rates will be in effect at the Blue[2] Hotel. For as little as $45 a day you can have a delightful room on the ocean side of the[3] hotel. This rate includes breakfast and dinner as well as the use of all our facilities.

Make plans now to[4] enjoy a vacation that you will never forget. A convenient reservation form is enclosed. Sincerely yours,[5]   [100]

579   Dear Jane: Thanks for the copy of *Tennis Anyone?* I started reading it after dinner last Sunday and did[1] not put it down until I had finished it.

I am already a better tennis player! Sincerely,   [38]

580   *The Importance of Shorthand Speed*

Grace Miller, in her position as secretary to a young executive, was required to take a great deal[1] of dictation. Two or three hours of dictation a day was not uncommon.

Grace found that at the end of the day[2] she was physically exhausted.

Her friend Donna Nelson had a similar position with another[3] executive in the same company. Donna didn't seem to work half as hard as Grace, and at the end of the day[4] she still had plenty of energy. In addition, she turned out much more work than Grace.

Why was Grace so tired and[5] Donna still energetic at the end of each day? The answer was shorthand speed. Grace had heard that executives[6] rarely dictate more than 80 words a minute; consequently, she did not bother to build her speed beyond that point.[7]

Thus, although her employer's rate of dictation was not very rapid, she had to strain constantly to keep up.[8] Because Grace was always writing at her top speed, her notes were often poorly written, so she had difficulty[9] reading them when she transcribed. As a result, taking dictation and transcribing it were both very hard work for[10] her.

Donna, on the other hand, had not been satisfied with a shorthand speed of 80 words a minute. She was[11] able to take over 100 words a minute and was still developing her shorthand speed two or three hours[12] a week. Donna's employer dictated almost as fast as Grace's, but Donna did not have to strain to take the[13] dictation.

She had a good reserve of shorthand speed; consequently, she could take dictation for long periods[14] of time without getting tired. Taking dictation and transcribing were easy and pleasant tasks for Donna.[15]

Follow Donna's example and develop your shorthand speed as far as possible. The faster you can write shorthand,[16] the easier taking dictation and reading your notes will be. [332]

CHAPTER 14

LESSON 66

582 Dear Mr. Waters: As you may know, we have been working very hard for the past three months to get ready for the[1] formal opening of our new restaurant on Monday, January 21. I am happy to say that[2] despite many problems and delays, it appears that we will be able to open on that date.

We want a[3] representative of the Chamber of Commerce to be with us on the evening of January 21[4] to take part in the opening ceremonies. Do you think this will be possible?

Several days ago we[5] invited the *Daily Tribune* to send a reporter to cover our opening.

May I hear from you as soon[6] as possible concerning the participation of the Chamber of Commerce. Very truly yours, [138]

Office-Style Dictation
583 (*As dictated*) Dear Miss White: We are very glad (make that, *of course, very glad*) to accept your cordial (no, *kind*) invitation to participate in the opening ceremonies of the Red Barn Restaurant on Monday, January 21. We will be happy to take part (change that to *the Chamber of Commerce is delighted to be able to be a part of*) such an event. We feel that your elegant restaurant (make that *new restaurant*) will be a welcome, much-

needed addition to Chicago, and we want to do everything in our power to help make it a commercial success.

Please (make that *will you please*) let me know if you would like to have someone from our organization make a presentation (say *short presentation*) or if you would simply like to have several of the chamber's representatives in attendance. It will be our pleasure to follow your wishes. Cordially yours,

583 (*As it would be transcribed*) Dear Miss White: We are, of course, very glad to accept your kind invitation to participate in the opening[1] ceremonies of the Red Barn Restaurant on Monday, January 21. The Chamber of Commerce[2] is delighted to be able to be a part of such an event. We feel that your elegant new restaurant[3] will be a welcome, much-needed addition to Chicago, and we want to do everything in our power[4] to help make it a commercial success.

Will you please let me know if you would like to have someone from our[5] organization make a short presentation or if you would simply like to have several of the chamber's[6] representatives in attendance. It will be our pleasure to follow your wishes. Cordially yours, [137]

585 Dear Miss White: We are, of course, very glad to accept your kind invitation to participate in the opening[1] ceremonies of the Red Barn Restaurant on Monday, January 21. The Chamber of Commerce[2] is delighted to be able to be a part of such an event. We feel that your elegant new restaurant[3] will be a welcome, much-needed addition to Chicago, and we want to do everything in our power[4] to help make it a commercial success.

Will you please let me know if you would like to have someone from our[5] organization make a short presentation or if you would simply like to have several of the chamber's[6] representatives in attendance. It will be our pleasure to follow your wishes. Cordially yours, [137]

586 Dear Mr. Waters: Thank you very much for your help at the grand opening of the Red Barn Restaurant in[1] Chicago. As you can well imagine, we were quite pleased with the large turnout of dignitaries from the city,[2] county, and state governments as well as the fine representation from the Chamber of Commerce.

We are looking[3] forward to many years of successful business operations here in Chicago's uptown area. Sincerely[4] yours, [81]

587 Dear Mr. Jones: I am considering enlarging our restaurant which I opened last year in the city of[1] Chicago. Since opening the restaurant, I have realized that the seating capacity is insufficient;[2] therefore, I want to add space for at least 100 tables.

In order to expand, we will have to apply for[3] a variance from the zoning ordinance. We want to expand to a point within 15 feet of the curb. The[4] zoning ordinance, which I have carefully studied, specifies that no building be placed closer than 20 feet[5] to the curb. When you have a moment, please look into this matter and let me know whether we will be able to[6] obtain such a variance.

112 Lesson 66

Very truly yours, [129]

588 Dear Mr. Bell: Haven't you often wished that the village of Bristol had a really fine restaurant that served[1] appetizing meals at prices that were not sky high? Well, that wish will shortly be fulfilled. On Monday, June 18, Jim[2] Smith and I will open the Bristol Steak House at 114 Main Street, which is just across the street from the Bristol[3] National Bank.

We will, of course, specialize in steaks of all kinds. However, we will also serve the finest fish[4] and poultry.

Enclosed is an invitation for you and your family to be our guests for dinner any day[5] after our opening on June 18. To be sure that we can accommodate you, make a reservation the[6] day before you plan to come. Our telephone number is 116-1181. Sincerely yours, [138]

589 Dear Miss White: Thank you for your letter asking about the possibility of obtaining a variance from[1] the city's zoning ordinance. I have looked into the matter carefully and have decided that it would not[2] be in our best interests to permit you to construct an addition to your restaurant which would extend[3] into the sidewalk area.

I suggest that you consider adding a second floor to the restaurant in[4] order to accommodate an extra 100 tables. This *appears** to be the simpler, more practical solution[5] to your problem.

If I can be of *help*† to you in the future, please call on me. Very truly yours, [118]

Also correct:
*seems
†assistance, aid

LESSON 67

594 Dear Mr. Leslie: In yesterday's newspaper I saw your advertisement about a management position[1] with Bennington Sweet Shops. The position sounds like an interesting one, and I would like to be considered an[2] applicant. I have had several years' experience in the restaurant business in Arkansas, but I have[3] never managed a shop of my own. Although I am a conscientious, competent, and dependable person,[4] I would need help in running a shop for several months.

I am enclosing a complete vita. When you have had[5] an opportunity to look over it, I hope you will call me. Sincerely yours,　　　　[115]

595 Dear Ms. Cook: If you are looking for a management opportunity with unlimited potential, we know[1] you will be interested in learning what Burlington's International Restaurants have to offer. When you[2] work for us, we do not ordinarily stop with your first promotion; we do not even stop with the second.[3] Because we are opening new restaurants almost weekly throughout the United States and Europe, we can[4] offer our managers unlimited opportunities.

At Burlington's, you can earn $10,000 during[5] your first year. It is not unusual for our top managers to earn as much as $30,000[6] after only a few years.

If you are interested in a management position in one of our pleasant[7] restaurants, fill out and return the enclosed card today. It could put you on the road to unlimited success.[8] Cordially yours,　　　　[162]

596 Dear Miss Harrington: Here is good news for you. Enclosed is a booklet of coupons which I am sure you will find[1] very useful during the coming month. The booklet is worth $8. It is being distributed only to[2] the residents of the area served by the American Food Market to help them reduce their food bills for[3] the month and to encourage them to shop in our store. All you need do is select the name-brand merchandise listed[4] on the coupons and present them at the checkout counter.

Take a few minutes to look over the booklet now, Miss[5] Harrington, and then take advantage of the good buys available only at our grocery store. Sincerely[6] yours,　　　　[121]

597 Dear Mr. Keith: As you know, the Kentucky Department of Health conducts a check of all restaurants in the state.[1] We try to visit every restaurant at least once a year.

When a restaurant is found to be in[2] violation of the health code, it is given one week to correct the problem. If it has not been corrected at that[3] time, the restaurant is fined. If it is not corrected after one month, its license is revoked.

Your new restaurant[4] in Lexington will be visited for the first time on Tuesday, February 3. After the initial[5] inspection, you may be visited at any time without notice. The necessity for this type of program[6] is evident. We must strive to keep high standards for all restaurants in our state. Very sincerely yours, [138]

598 Mr. Jackson: As you know, Christmas is only a few weeks away, and we should be making plans to hire[1] temporary help to take care of the increased business that the Christmas season always brings. May I suggest that you take[2] the following steps immediately:

1. Talk to the local high school principal and ask him to refer to[3] us any boys and girls who would be interested in working for the Wilson Supermarket after school from[4] December 15 to 24.

2. Beginning November 1, place an ad in the newspaper soliciting[5] temporary employees.

If you have any other suggestions for meeting this Christmas help problem, please[6] let me have them. James Abbey [125]

599 Dear Mr. Davis: It is a pleasure to tell you that your new restaurant passed the State Department of Health[1] examination; you satisfied all our requirements easily.

Enclosed is a placard that you should *display**,* in[2] a prominent place in your restaurant at all times. As you will *note,*† you have received the rating "Satisfactory,"[3] which is the top rating that we give. If we had an "Excellent" rating, your new restaurant would certainly[4] have won it.

Please keep up the high standards which you have established for your restaurant. Remember that the Department[5] of Health may visit you again unannounced at any time. Cordially yours, [114]

Also correct:
*leave
†see

LESSON 68

603 Dear Miss Long: Just one year ago the East Side Community Club organized the first food cooperative

in[1] the city. In that short year the cooperative has grown into one of the largest, most respected[2] organizations in the Midwest. Nearly 1,000 members belong to the club.

Why has this organization been[3] such a big success? The answer is easy: We coordinate our efforts in order to keep our food bills to[4] the very minimum for our members.

For a small monthly service fee and one day's work per month, you, too, can be[5] a member of this well-run organization. If you would like more information, just call me at[6] 555-6611 or write to me at my office at 1900 First Avenue. Cordially yours, [138]

604 Dear Ms. Wilson: I am interested indeed! I would like to belong to the food cooperative that you[1] described in your letter of March 10; it sounds like a wonderful organization. If there is anything I[2] can do to lower my food bill, which is currently almost $200 a month, I certainly want to[3] do it.

Will you please send me all the details along with a membership application blank which I will complete[4] and return to you immediately.

I do have one problem, however. I understand that all members must[5] spend one day a month shopping for food products for the cooperative. Naturally, I want to cooperate,[6] but I work from nine to five on weekdays; therefore, I would be able to shop only on the weekends. Will this[7] be satisfactory? I am looking forward to hearing from you soon. Very truly yours, [157]

605 Dear Miss Long: Thank you

for replying to my letter so promptly. It is with pleasure that I send you an[1] application blank for membership in our food cooperative. An application blank is enclosed.

If you return[2] the completed form to me before the end of April, you will be able to start using the services of[3] our organization on May 1. However, if you apply after April 30, you will have to wait[4] until June to begin taking advantage of the food bargains offered each month to our members.

In your letter you[5] indicated that you would not be able to work any weekday for the organization. As the wholesale[6] markets we use are not open on Saturdays, Sundays, and holidays, I'm afraid you will not be able to[7] serve the required one day each month as a buyer. However, you have two alternatives:

1. You may make arrangements[8] with another member to take care of your obligation to us, or

2. You may pay an additional[9] fee directly to us.

Either decision is perfectly acceptable to us. We look forward to receiving[10] your application soon. Very cordially yours, [210]

606 Dear Ms. Wilson: Enclosed is the completed application *blank** for membership in the food cooperative.[1] I am sorry that I was not able to return the form to you before the end of April. I was trying[2] to get one of the regular members of the organization to take my place as a buyer one day each[3] month. I am sorry to say, Ms. Wilson, that I have not been able to find *anyone†* who can do this for me.[4]

Therefore, it will be necessary for me to pay an additional fee each month. Will you please let me know how[5] much this fee will be. When I hear from you, I will send you a check for the month of June. Sincerely yours, [118]

Also correct:

*form

†a person, anybody

LESSON 69

610 Gentlemen: I have just finished reading your company's new publication, *The Backyard Vegetable Garden.[1]* The book was given to me as a Christmas gift, and, frankly, I did not believe that I would find it very[2] interesting. After reading the foreword and only a few pages of the text, however, I realized that it[3] was full of practical, sensible hints on how to turn extra yard space into a productive vegetable[4] garden.

Naturally, I plan to start my own garden as soon as spring arrives. I will be looking forward to[5] other publications from your company. Cordially yours, [111]

611 Dear Mr. Lee: Thank you for giving us your opinion of our new book, *The Backyard Vegetable Garden.* We[1] are happy that you enjoyed the book and that it has helped you with your gardening problems. We believe that people[2] all over the country will enjoy the book just as much as you did.

As you will see on page 18 of the[3] enclosed catalog, we publish several other books of interest to the home gardener. We think you will be[4] particularly interested in our latest publication, *Making Yard Work Fun.* Why not use the attached[5] card to order *a copy.* Yours very truly, [109]

612   Dear Consumer: We are happy to announce that our food store has been chosen as one of only 50 in the[1] South to take part in a national program which we hope will eventually lower food prices while at the[2] same time give customers faster, more efficient service.

On Wednesday, July 15, our store will inaugurate[3] this unique program. On that date none of our products will carry individual price tags. Rather, each will[4] be marked with a special computer code which will be used at the checkout counter. It will automatically[5] total your bill many times faster than the most efficient, well-trained clerk. You will still be able to know the[6] individual prices of the items; they will appear on the shelf directly below the items.

The savings[7] will come about in this way: We will no longer have to take the time to mark the price on each item. We will be[8] able to handle far more customers with greater efficiency. Thus these savings, which should be sizable, can[9] be passed on to you, the consumer.

We hope you will enjoy this new way of buying groceries. We look forward[10] to having you visit us in our store soon. Sincerely yours, [211]

613   Dear Fred: Best wishes on your twenty-fifth birthday. As a birthday gift, I am giving you a year's subscription to[1] the Fruit-of-the-Month Club. This month you will receive a basket of apples, and each month thereafter you will receive[2] a basket of whatever fruit is in season.

I hope you enjoy your gift. Yours very truly,   [57]

116   Lesson 70

614   Dear Mr. Hart: For many years I have shopped at the General Food Market, and I have always found your shop to[1] be one of the best, most economical stores in town.

When you announced that your store was taking part in a[2] federally sponsored program to test whether or not the new electronic computer could be *used** to total[3] food bills, I was hesitant to express my approval.

I agree that the method should be faster and more[4] efficient, but I have actually found it to be a hindrance in my shopping. On a number of occasions[5] I have had serious problems because of a discrepancy between the prices on the items and those charged[6] me by the computer.

If this *problem*† is not solved, I doubt that the program will be faster, more accurate, and[7] more efficient. Very truly yours,   [147]
Also correct:
*utilized
†trouble

LESSON 70

617   Dear Dr. Yale: According to reports in the newspapers, there has been a recent federal government[1] regulation which limits the use of special dyes contained in food products and that all manufacturers must[2] abide by this regulation starting the first of the year.

My organization, the National Food Company,[3] produces boxed cake mixes. These mixes, which are sold in major supermarkets throughout the country, contain red,[4] yellow, and blue dyes. I am wondering, therefore, whether this new regulation affects us. When you have an[5] opportunity, please let me have your opinion. Cordially yours, [112]

618 Dear Ms. Wilson: Enclosed is a copy of the complete set of guidelines which the food and drug division of the[1] federal government has developed for dye content in food products. As you will see, there are several new,[2] rather sweeping restrictions which definitely affect the amount and type of dyes that food products may contain.[3]

Please read the guidelines carefully. It is quite possible that the new regulations may have an effect on your[4] operation and that you will have to obtain different dyes to substitute for some of those you currently[5] use.

If I can be of further help, please write me. Sincerely yours, [112]

619 Dear Dr. Yale: A few weeks ago I read that new federal regulations limit the type and amount of[1] dyes which can be used in food products.

For the past year I have been concerned about the dyes used in foods, and I would[2] like to check on three particular products which may contain an excessive amount of dye. The labels from these[3] three brand-name products are enclosed.

Will you please check them and let me know if the dyes used in them meet the federal[4] regulations. Thank you for your help, Dr. Yale; I appreciate it. Sincerely yours, [96]

620 Dear Mr. Fox: We have carefully checked the labels you sent us and have found that all three products meet the federal[1] government's current regulations.

The manufacturers of two of the products recently changed the type[2] of dyes used. The manufacturer of the third product has eliminated the use of dyes altogether.[3]

If you have further questions about the new federal regulations, please let me know. I will be happy to[4] answer them for you. Very truly yours, [87]

621 Dear Mrs. Jerome: When the James Supermarket started as a little dairy store about 70 years[1] ago, our specialty was butter. We sold only the highest quality butter.

Though times have changed and we have grown[2] into a major food store, we are still as fussy about the quality of our butter as we were then. Our[3] butter has received the highest rating from the government that butter can receive. It more than meets government[4] standards for body, flavor, and aroma.

We know you will enjoy our butter, so get a supply the next time[5] you visit the James Supermarket. We are open every weekday from nine to five. On Sundays we are[6] open from nine to one. Sincerely yours, [127]

622 Dear Mrs. Jackson: Everyone talks about high food prices. We at the *Daily Times* are doing something[1] about them. Every day our food editors will suggest to you a different kitchen-tested recipe that[2] your entire family will enjoy and that will at the same time help you keep your food costs down.

All you have to do[3] is dial 116-8181 and have a pencil and paper ready. A pleasant voice will read the day's[4] suggested recipe to you and give you whatever special instructions are necessary to use it.[5]

Dial the *Daily Times* food department now and delight your family with a delicious, inexpensive meal.

This[6] is just another service that we are glad to offer to the citizens of Winfield.

By the way, Mrs.[7] Jackson, do you enjoy home delivery of the *Daily Times*? We will be glad to arrange it for you if you will[8] fill out and return the enclosed card. Sincerely yours, [170]

623 *Don't Waste the Pauses*

Don Gray took dictation from two executives, each of whom had dictating peculiarities. Mr. Barnes[1] had his thoughts well organized, and he dictated quite rapidly. He seldom paused for any length of time. To get[2] his dictation, Don had to keep his mind closely on his writing.

Ms. Davis, however, dictated at an[3] irregular pace. She would dictate a sentence or two quite rapidly and then stop to think. She would often pause for[4] a number of seconds, groping for just the right word.

During these pauses, Don could simply have sat and waited for[5] Ms. Davis to resume her dictation. But this sitting and waiting would quickly have become boring and would have[6] wasted time.

Don was wise; he used the time provided by the pauses in dictation to read over his notes and[7] make them easier to transcribe. For example, he improved any outlines that he had not written very clearly[8] because the dictation was rapid. He inserted punctuation and indicated paragraphs. He circled[9] words that he would look up because he was not sure of the spelling.

As a result, he was able to tran-

scribe[10] his notes much more rapidly than he would have if he had simply wasted the time while Ms. Davis was thinking.[11]

When your employer pauses in dictation, don't waste the time. Spend it profitably reading over your notes. [239]

CHAPTER 15

LESSON 71

625 Gentlemen: For the past three or four years I have been making regularly scheduled trips to the East Coast. My last[1] trip was only a week ago. Each time I have to change planes in either Dallas or Atlanta. There is always[2] a layover of one or two hours in these cities. This, of course, makes me lose several hours of my time on each[3] trip.

I am wondering if the city government has ever made an application to have one of the airlines[4] fly directly to the East Coast. I am sure that there are many business executives in the area[5] who would appreciate this service very much. It would be a great convenience for me if I could fly[6] directly to the East Coast without having to change planes. I hope you will speak to the authorities to see if we[7] can get this service for the travelers from our area.

If you would like me to help in any way, I will[8] be glad to do whatever I can. Sincerely yours, [170]

Office-Style Dictation

626 *(As dictated)* Dear Ms. Cunningham: The city of Brownsville is seeking (make that *looking for*; oh, change that back to *seeking*) new air service to the East, and we are asking for the support of all interested citizens in helping us obtain this service. For 25 years Brownsville has been served by two airlines —Valley Airlines, a small company that operates (change that to *flies*; oh, leave it *operates*) within the state and General Airlines, a major airline that provides interstate service to Chicago, Dallas, and Atlanta. We have never had direct flights to the cities of Washington, Philadelphia, New York, and several other eastern metropolises (no, *cities*; oh, leave it *metropolises*).

We hope that we can convince both the federal authorities and a major airline that Brownsville can support another airline to supply service to the East. In order to help us with our presentation to the government, we are conducting a study of the needs (make that *requirements*; oh, leave it *needs*) of several large business concerns in the area. Will you please fill out the enclosed questionnaire...

626 *(As it would be transcribed)* Dear Ms. Cunningham: The city of Brownsville is seeking new air service to the East, and we are asking for the[1] support of all interested citizens in helping us obtain this service. For 25 years Brownsville has[2] been served by two airlines—Valley Airlines, a small company that operates within the state and General Airlines,[3] a major airline that provides interstate service to Chicago, Dallas, and Atlanta. We have never[4] had direct flights to the cities of Washington, Philadelphia, New York, and several other eastern[5] metropolises.

We hope that we can convince

both the federal authorities and a major airline that[6] Brownsville can support another airline to supply service to the East. In order to help us with our presentation[7] to the government, we are conducting a study of the needs of several large business concerns in the[8] area. Will you please fill out the enclosed questionnaire...   [170]

628 Dear Ms. Cunningham: The city of Brownsville is seeking new air service to the East, and we are asking for the[1] support of all interested citizens in helping us obtain this service.

For 25 years Brownsville has[2] been served by two airlines—Valley Airlines, a small company that operates within the state and General Airlines,[3] a major airline that provides interstate service to Chicago, Dallas, and Atlanta. We have never[4] had direct flights to the cities of Washington, Philadelphia, New York, and several other eastern[5] metropolises.

We hope that we can convince both the federal authorities and a major airline that[6] Brownsville can support another airline to supply service to the East.

In order to help us with our presentation[7] to the government, we are conducting a study of the needs of several large business concerns in the[8] area. Will you please fill out the enclosed two-page questionnaire concerning the travel requirements of your company[9] executives for the next two or three months. This could be a great help to us in obtaining this new service,[10] Ms Cunningham. Very truly yours,   [207]

629 Dear Miss Simms: It is heartening to know that the Chamber of Commerce is taking action to obtain air service[1] from Brownsville to cities in the East. I have long believed that this type of service was needed and would be used[2] regularly by business executives in this area.

Enclosed is the completed questionnaire you sent to[3] me. As you will note, three or four of the executives of our company will be making regular trips to[4] Washington, Philadelphia, and New York in the coming year. It is now necessary for us to schedule[5] a two-hour layover in Atlanta. If we can obtain direct service, we will be able to save several[6] hours' travel time on each trip. I do not need to tell you how valuable this service would be for us. When a[7] federal body decides to hold a hearing on this matter, I will be glad to testify before it.[8] Cordially yours, [162]

630 Dear Ms. Carpenter: As you have probably read in the newspapers during the past few months, my company, Central[1] Airlines, is trying to get approval to serve the citizens of Jackson. We have applied for routes from Jackson[2] to Dallas, Atlanta, and Houston. However, we have not yet been able to get permission to land at[3] the Jackson airport.

It has occurred to us that we might be able to operate at the Green County airport,[4] which is located only three or four miles from the regular commercial airport. As you know, however, we[5] need the permission of the county commissioners to do so. As a commissioner for Green County, you are[6] aware of the value of the service our airline could

provide to the area. May I have the opportunity[7] to discuss this matter with you? Very truly yours, [151]

631 Dear Mr. Green: If you have ever gone to Florida on the Southern Comet, you know everything on that train[1] is deluxe from the clean, comfortable seats to the excellent food and service in our dining car.

Even though[2] we are known for our good passenger service, we make no money from it. It amounts to less than 1 percent of[3] our total revenue. But as long as we move passengers, we want to keep our good name with those who travel with[4] us.

Moving freight is the profitable side of our business. We do so well in moving freight that we have increased[5] our earnings per share by 102 percent over the last five years.

Whether you wish us to take you to any[6] one of the southern states that we serve or to deliver your freight there, you can be sure you will receive the fastest,[7] most economical service of which we are capable. Sincerely yours, [154]

632 Dear Mr. O'Neill: Will it be possible for you or one of your executives to attend the federal[1] hearing on the new air service between Brownsville and the large cities in the East? The hearing will be held in[2] Washington on Wednesday, February 23. As you know, the Chamber of Commerce has been working for many months[3] to *obtain** this new service for our city. There is one major airline applying for the new routes, and we would[4] like to give it our support.

In order to present our case effectively, we must have testimony from[5] several executives whose *companies*† would make use of this service on a regular basis. Because your[6] company is one of the major users of the service, we would like you to testify at the hearing. Please let[7] me know if you can do so; a stamped, self-addressed envelope is enclosed for your convenience. Sincerely yours,[8]   [160]

Also correct:
*get
†organizations, businesses

LESSON 72

637 Dear Traveler: The next time you plan a vacation in Europe, why not plan to see the rural countryside by[1] rail. If you have ever had the experience of flying from one European city to another, didn't[2] you feel cheated because you were deprived of the opportunity of seeing the open countryside? If[3] you travel by train instead of by plane, you will have ample opportunity to see the sights in each country.[4]

For a small one-time charge, you will have two weeks of first-class travel over any of the regular train routes of[5] Europe. All you have to do is present your card to one of the station attendants, and you will have the "best seat[6] in the house" to view the great beauty of the open country of Europe. The card is good 24 hours a day.[7] Call your travel agent for full details. Sincerely yours,   [150]

638 Dear Consumer: Don't buy our oil! This may sound like an extraordinary statement for an oil company to[1] make, and it is, of course. But we don't mean to ask you to stop buying Louisiana gasoline and oil[2] altogether.

What we would like you to do is conserve our nation's shrinking supply of oil. Make sure that when you use[3] your car, the trip is worth the gasoline you use. When you drive, keep well under the stated speed limits. You will not[4] only conserve gasoline, but you will also be making a contribution to safer driving.

Incidentally,[5] when you do stop for gasoline, be sure that it is the finest available—Louisiana[6] gasoline. In our opinion, we have the best products and service in the world. Cordially yours,   [137]

639 Dear Mr. Case: On Monday and Tuesday, November 3 and 4, there will be a national conference on the[1] conservation of energy. The meeting will be held in the Lexington Room of the Circle Hotel in Reno,[2] Nevada. The sessions will begin at 9 a.m. and last until 4 p.m. each day. Many prominent[3] people will take part in the panel discussions.

The attendance should be over 2,000 and we believe there[4] is a good chance that it might reach 2,500.

Won't you join us at this meeting. The stamped, self-addressed[5] envelope enclosed is for your convenience in letting us know that you will attend. Your attendance will be[6] appreciated. Sincerely yours,   [126]

640 Dear Ms. Willis: A few days ago I reserved a seat on yesterday's Central Airlines Flight 23 from Atlanta,[1] Georgia, to Wichita, Kansas. Yesterday morning I left home about an hour earlier than I[2] ordinarily would, but I experienced great difficulty en route to the terminal. The traffic was[3] unusually heavy at that time of the day. When I finally arrived at the terminal, I realized that[4] it was very late and that my plane was probably already loaded and would be departing shortly.

At the gate[5] I found that the doors had already been closed, but the plane had not left the gate. One of the attendants there spoke to[6] the captain on the phone, and very soon the doors reopened enabling me to board the plane.

Because I was[7] on my way to a crucial government meeting that was of utmost importance to me and my company, it[8] was of vital importance for me to get on that particular plane. Needless to say, Ms. Willis, I am deeply[9] indebted to the attendant, the captain, and Central Airlines. May I take this opportunity to say[10] "thank you" in an official way. Sincerely yours,   [209]

641 Dear Mr. Parker: A few days ago I called your office and requested you to send a truck to pick up[1] several packages that were to be delivered to our Charleston office. The poor service that I received is very[2] difficult to understand.

The truck driver came to my office twice, but he would not take the packages either[3] time because there was some *problem** with the order form. On the third trip he picked up the packages, but he[4] apparently lost one of them because it was not delivered to our Charleston office.

This missing package is very[5] important; it contains papers that are invaluable. I talked with the people in your tracing department,[6] and although they were *polite*,[†] their ef-

ficiency left much to be desired. Frankly, I felt that they were not really[7] concerned with my problem. I want a competent, responsible person to trace this package, find it, and return[8] it to me promptly. Please give this matter your personal attention. Sincerely yours,   [176]
Also correct:
*trouble
†nice

LESSON 73

645 Dear Friend: For some time the Chamber of Commerce of Port Arthur has been considering the establishment of a[1] transportation museum for the city. At a meeting several months ago, the Chamber of Commerce[2] appointed a committee to investigate this possibility. From its inception the idea was to[3] include authentic models of early automobiles, trains, and planes. The committee has decided that such a[4] museum would be a very worthwhile project for the residents of our city.

We plan to construct a small[5] building on city-owned land near the central business district. Eventually we hope to construct a larger[6] building in the same area.

We are now soliciting funds to help with the initial construction. If you[7] would like to contribute to this project, we will be happy to add your name to our list of contributors. A[8] donation in any amount from $1 to $1,000 or more will be greatly appreciated[9] by our committee. Cordially yours,   [187]

646 Dear Miss Collins: As you know, several months ago we began soliciting money to construct a transportation[1] museum for the city of Port Arthur. To date, we have collected more than 50 percent of the[2] amount necessary to construct the first building.

We are very proud of this accomplishment, but we frankly[3] need help in raising the remaining amount. Will you please give this matter some consideration and let us have[4] your ideas in the next week or two. We hope to complete our fund-raising campaign by the end of the year. Yours[5] very truly, [103]

647 Dear Mr. Gates: I am planning to fly to Harrisburg on Thursday, December 13, on General Airlines[1] Flight 1616 to help prepare the company's budget for the coming year. Will you please make local arrangements[2] for my stay. I would like to have a single room for December 13, 14, and 15. The Johnson Motel,[3] which is just a few blocks from the Harrisburg office, will be all right with me.

Please do not feel obligated[4] to meet my plane, Mr. Gates. Because I will be arriving at 2 a.m., I will take a taxi directly[5] to the motel.

I am looking forward to seeing the members of the Harrisburg branch once again. I hope it[6] will be possible for the accounting department staff to be my guests for luncheon on one of the three days that[7] I will be there. Yours very truly, [147]

648 Dear Mr. Wilson: I will be arriving in Fitchburg on January 30 at 4 p.m. on Central[1] Airlines Flight 193. Will it be possible for someone from the main office to meet me at the airport and[2] drive me to the Hotel White?

I will be attending the reception for our retiring president, Ms. Jane Smith,[3] from 7 to 10 p.m. I will also need transportation back to the air terminal after the reception.[4]

Thank you for your help. I would appreciate this favor very much. Sincerely yours, [96]

649 Dear Ms. Jones: As you know, two members of my department will be retiring on August 1. The other members[1] of my department and I are planning to pay tribute to them at a formal reception and dinner on Sunday,[2] July 25, in the Blue Room of the Hotel President at six in the evening. I hope you will be[3] able to attend this memorable event.

Bill Green has been with our *company**[*]* for over 30 years and[4] has served in the accounting department for 18 years. When we became a part of the Amtrak operation,[5] Bill became head of the accounting department.

Mary Smith has been with the company for 25 years. She[6] served in the finance, marketing, and office services departments. Both Bill and Mary have *rendered*[†] invaluable[7] service to the company.

Will you please let me know by June 10 if you will be able to attend the[8] reception and dinner. Very truly yours, [167]

Also correct:
*organization, business
†given

LESSON 74

653 Dear Commuter: As you probably are aware, for the past three years the Main Street Transportation Terminal has[1] not been able to satisfy the demands placed on it by the large number of people who pass through the facility[2] daily. The Transit Authority is pleased to announce that we will begin remodeling and enlarging[3] the terminal in April. When we finish the job about a year later, the terminal will be able[4] to handle almost twice the traffic that now passes through its portals.

When the Main Street Transportation Terminal[5] was proposed 25 years ago, there was a great deal of doubt about the feasibility of locating[6] such a facility in the area. We are happy to report that as of last year the terminal was[7] the busiest transportation facility on the East Coast.

We look forward to serving you and the other[8] commuters in the years to come. Yours very truly,

[170]

654 Dear Commuter: About six months ago the Transit Authority began a major project which, when completed,[1] will double the size and capacity of the Main Street Transportation Terminal. We are pleased to announce[2] that the project is on schedule; the new wing will open officially next spring.

During the next three months, however,[3] we will have to make two major changes. The Third Avenue entrance will be closed between Main Street and Broadway[4] beginning September 1, and the Park Avenue entrance will be open only during rush hours. We are asking[5] commuters to enter and leave by the Second Avenue entrance during this time.

We know that you will enjoy[6]

using the enlarged terminal when it is open next year, and we hope that the temporary changes will[7] not seriously inconvenience you. In the meantime, if you have any questions about our present[8] enlarging plans, please write us. Sincerely yours,

[167]

655 Dear Mr. Kenney: Two weeks ago my son brought my car into your repair shop for a general maintenance[1] checkup. I have had my car checked in May each year since I purchased it three years ago. My relationship with your[2] company has always been excellent.

When my son picked up the car, he was given a bill for $250,[3] which he reluctantly paid. When he came home, he showed the bill to me, and I was as upset as he was.[4] When I went over the itemized statement, I simply couldn't believe the number of things that had been done. New[5] brake linings, a new fan belt, and new spark plugs had been installed.

I have never had a bill for more than $100[6] for general maintenance in the past. Frankly, I feel that you have taken advantage of us, and you[7] can be sure that in the future we will take our business elsewhere. Yours truly, [154]

656 Dear Mr. Keith: Your distressing letter arrived in today's mail. For many years we have had a pleasant,[1] mutually satisfactory relationship, and the loss of your friendship is a severe blow to us. We are[2] very much concerned that you feel you were overcharged by our repair shop.

I have checked with our manager, Mr.[3] Kenneth Gates, and he showed me a form which was signed by your son when he brought the car in for general maintenance[4] service. The form authorized us to make all the repairs that were listed on the bill.

Therefore, we adjusted all parts[5] which were loose and replaced those which were worn. We installed new spark plugs and replaced the brake linings. Incidentally,[6] all the items on the list are included in the suggested maintenance schedule for your car at the[7] 36-month checkup. Your car is now in top running order, and I am sure you will not need to bring it in for[8] servicing for many months to come.

Although I feel that we were justified in the charges that we made, I am[9] deeply sorry that we are losing your friendship. We want to do everything in our power, Mr. Keith, to[10] regain your confidence. Won't you come in the next time you are in the area and talk over the matter with us.[11] Very truly yours, [224]

657 Dear Miss Stern: As you probably know, in the past 12 months there has been a rapid rise in the number of automobile[1] accidents in and around the city of Greenburg. The transportation committee of the Chamber of[2] Commerce would like to initiate a project designed to reduce the number of accidents in the city.[3]

Because you are an outstanding teacher of driver education in one of our local high schools, you are the[4] *person** we have decided to ask to head this project.

We are sure, Miss Stern, that you will have many good ideas[5] on how we can make driving safer in Greenburg. If you will take the responsibility of serving as[6] head of a com-

mittee to *handle*† this project, we will be very grateful. Very truly yours, [137]
Also correct:
*one
†lead, head up

LESSON 75

660 Dear Mr. Pulaski: As you may have heard, the city of Plattsburg is hoping to build a perimeter road[1] around the outskirts of town during the next two or three years, and we need your help.

For some time east-west traffic has[2] been routed through the main streets of Plattsburg causing much noise, congestion, and pollution. While north-south traffic has been[3] routed through the suburbs, there is still more congestion than drivers can tolerate. A loop around the city would[4] provide cross-country travelers with a route that would bypass the city.

In order to finance construction of[5] the highway, we must obtain the approval of the county governments in both counties through which the highway will[6] pass. May we count on you to present our case in a special report to the Jones County commissioners? We will[7] appreciate your support. Cordially yours, [148]

661 Dear Miss Lang: I was very glad to receive your letter concerning the highway planned for Plattsburg. I am convinced[1] that this type of highway, which will not be too expensive to build, is necessary to relieve the congestion[2] and pollution which is adversely affecting business in the central commercial district of Plattsburg.

I will[3] certainly give my full support to the project, Miss Lang. When you have completed your preliminary plans, please[4] let me have a copy; I will present them to the Jones County commissioners with a covering report of[5] my own. Please keep me posted concerning your progress. Sincerely yours,   [113]

662 Dear Miss Mild: Thank you for your interest in the position that is open in the marketing department of[1] The General Import and Export Company. I am happy to give you the details of the job.

We are looking[2] for a person to be a marketing manager for our West Coast office. The person who is employed in[3] this job will be responsible for all our marketing operations in seven western cities. This person[4] will supervise an advertising staff of five people, a marketing research staff of four people, two clerks, and[5] four secretaries.

It will be necessary for the new manager to visit all of the major cities[6] where we operate at least twice a year. In addition, the new manager must attend the company's two-week[7] national sales meeting held in Los Angeles each year.

The main responsibility of the marketing[8] manager is to build up our import and export business on the West Coast. If you are interested in applying[9] for the position, please fill out the enclosed application blank and return it in the stamped, self-addressed[10] envelope which is also enclosed. When we receive it, we will promptly schedule an interview for you with our[11] personnel director, Ms. Mary Green. Very truly yours,   [230]

663 Dear Ms. Duffy: Did you know that over 10 million Americans changed their addresses last year? And did you know[1] that over $50 million was claimed for damages caused by their moving companies? These startling facts were[2] revealed in a recent study on the mobility of Americans.

Millions of people move each year in[3] order to obtain better jobs, to get to a better climate, or to satisfy other personal requirements.[4] But why are so many of them dissatisfied with the service they receive from their movers? Some of their[5] dissatisfaction can be blamed on unusual circumstances or accidents, but most of it must be blamed on movers[6] who do not take a personal interest in their clients.

When you must move for any reason in the future, let[7] the National Moving Company handle all the details for you. In a recent survey we were named the most[8] dependable, reliable mover in the East. The main reason for this designation, we feel, is that our[9] company makes it a policy to take a personal interest in its customers. If any of your[10] furnishings are damaged during a move, we settle all claims in a few days. We never close the books on a job until[11] the customer is completely satisfied.

Our telephone number, Ms. Duffy, is 116-1161.[12] Try us the next time you are contemplating a move. Sincerely yours,   [253]

664 *What Would You Do?*
Most secretaries have some problems come up from time to time. The following are actual cases submitted[1] by secretaries. After you

read each one, think what you might have done. The answers are given at the end.

1. Suppose[2] you work in a small department with only three secretaries. You have made an appointment with someone from[3] another department for your coffee break in the lobby drugstore. Just before you are ready to leave, you find[4] that the other secretaries are leaving too. It is too late to telephone your friend. Would you:

a. Go anyway[5] on the chance the telephones won't ring?

b. Wait until the other secretaries come back and suggest that your friend[6] go with you for a second cup?

c. Forget the whole thing this time and stay at your desk?

2. What would you do if you[7] were walking through another department which was apparently unattended and one of the telephones rang?[8]

a. Answer the telephone and say, "No one is here."

b. Answer the telephone, take a message, and leave it with[9] your initials and extension number indicated.

c. Let the telephone ring.

3. A conference is to[10] be held among executives of your firm at 2 p.m. You are gathering all the information necessary[11] for this conference. One letter from a firm in your city that should be in your files just isn't there. You[12] check with three other people who often go to your files, but they say they haven't removed it. This letter has[13] information that is absolutely essential to the success of the conference.

The secretary who was[14] faced with this problem was able to solve it even though the letter could not be found. We'll tell you what she did; but,[15] before we do, what would you do?

4. While your employer has stepped out of the office for a few minutes, one of[16] his superiors stops by your desk to ask for some information you feel is confidential. Would you:

a. Give[17] it to him?

b. Tell him you don't know?

c. Explain that your employer will be back in a few minutes, and you feel[18] he has a better grasp of the information?

Answers

1.   c. In the future, try to work out a schedule for[19] breaks so you will know who is going at what time.

2.   b. Answer the telephone, take a message, and leave it with your[20] initials.

3.   After checking every possible place, this secretary telephoned the secretary of the[21] person who sent the letter and explained her predicament. She told her the approximate date on which the letter[22] was written, and asked her to dictate the necessary information from her carbon copy. Then the[23] information was typed and marked "Copy" so that the data would be available for the conference.

4.   c. Explain[24] that your employer will be back in a few minutes.

[490]

CHAPTER 16

LESSON 76

666   Dear Mr. Miller: We are considering replacing some of our typewriters at Central High School. The

last time[1] we replaced machines was three or four years ago, and some of them are in poor condition at this time.

We have been[2] told that your organization now sells several makes of typewriters. Will you please let us have any information[3] that is available on the design and operation of each of the machines you sell. We would also[4] like to know the prices of the various models and whether you allow a quantity discount to school[5] districts like ours.

Thank you very much for your help. Sincerely yours, [112]

Office-Style Dictation
667 *(As dictated)* Dear Dr. Sloan: Thank you for your letter requesting information about the cost of replacing and repairing (make that *repairing and replacing*) some of the typewriters in your school. I am happy to answer your questions about our used and new (change that to *new and used*) typewriters.

Our company handles several models including one with a 10-inch carriage and one with a 13-inch carriage. We also have both small and large (oh, make that *large and small*) typefaces which are interchangeable, of course. Each of these is fully described on the enclosed circular.

If you decide to purchase several machines at one time...

667 *(As if it would be transcribed)* Dear Dr. Sloan: Thank you for your letter requesting information about the cost of repairing and replacing[1] some of the typewriters in your school. I am happy to answer your questions about our new and used typewriters.[2]

Our company handles several models including one with a 10-inch carriage and one with a[3] 13-inch carriage. We also have both large and small typefaces which are interchangeable, of course. Each of these is[4] fully described on the enclosed circular.

If you decide to purchase several machines at one time... [98]

669 Dear Dr. Sloan: Thank you for your letter requesting information about the cost of your replacing some of[1] the typewriters in your school. I am happy to answer your questions about our new typewriters.

Our company[2] handles several models including one with a 10-inch carriage and one with a 13-inch carriage. We[3] also have both small and large typefaces which are interchangeable, of course. Each of these is fully described on the[4] enclosed circular.

If you decide to purchase several machines at one time, there would indeed be a quantity[5] discount. The local school district is not subject to any sales taxes whatever. Sincerely yours, [118]

670 Dear Mr. Miller: Enclosed is an order for three self-correcting typewriters to be used in the office[1] services laboratory of our high school. As you will note, we are ordering one Model A, one Model B,[2] and one Model C. We believe that by purchasing different models, we will be able to give our students[3] an opportunity to learn to use the special features of each of them.

Please deliver the machines to me[4] here at the high school, but send the bill to the school account-

ing department. Very truly yours,
[97]

671 Gentlemen: Several days ago we received in stock the new Model 121 offset duplicator from[1] the General Office Machine Manufacturing Company. I know you will be interested in seeing[2] the attractive, high-quality work it produces. This letter itself was actually printed on the[3] Model 121. Notice how clear and crisp the type is with no telltale smudges or indistinct letters.

The new[4] Model 121 is much smaller than comparable models; yet it costs no more than the old-fashioned machines. The[5] Model 121 is easy to install, easy to operate, and easy to clean.

Why not come to our[6] showroom and see for yourself all the distinctive new features of the Model 121. When you see it in[7] operation, we know you will want one for your office. Yours very truly, [153]

672 Dear Mrs. Rogers: Several months ago I purchased a Model 121 offset duplicator from your[1] company. It operated efficiently for some time, but during the past month, it has not been giving[2] satisfactory service. I have had your regular serviceman, Mr. Sam Smith, here on three occasions, and each[3] time he left saying that the machine was in good working order. Shortly after each of his visits, however,[4] the machine was again out of repair.

I am sorry to have to make this report, but I believe that the[5] quality of Mr. Smith's work is substandard. Will you please ask someone else to come to my office as soon as[6] possible to repair or replace the machine.

673 Dear Mr. Winters: Most organizations share a common problem. They must move paperwork with maximum speed[1] into the mails. However, every organization has its own internal and external mailing needs.[2] This means that every organization has a special problem that requires a special solution.

For more[3] than 50 years the Johnson Office Equipment Company has been solving paper-flow problems in businesses[4] of all sizes. If you have trouble with paper flow into and out of your mail room, we would welcome the chance to[5] help you solve it.

May we send one of our engineers to discuss your mailing problems? You will be placing yourself[6] under no obligation. Sincerely yours, [128]

674 Dear Mrs. Cunningham: I was quite disturbed to learn from your letter that the new Model 121 offset[1] duplicator you purchased from us has not been giving satisfactory service. I am also sorry that our[2] repairman, Sam Smith, did not make satisfactory repairs each time he visited your office. I have discussed[3] this with Mr. Smith, who is one of our best mechanics. He *tells** me that he believes your duplicator has[4] several major design problems which have caused the malfunction. Under the circumstances, I am arranging for[5] a representative of the General Office Machine Manufacturing Company to come to your[6] office next week to examine your duplicator.

Let me assure you, Mrs. Cunningham, that we will get your[7] *machine†* in top working order, or we will replace it with another machine. Yours very truly, [157]

Also correct:
*told, said to
†duplicator

LESSON 77

679 Dear Mr. Williams: In June, I will be moving to Des Moines, Iowa, to open a neighborhood office[1] supply store at 1440 West Street, and I would like to open an account with your organization.

I[2] foresee the need to charge as much as $5,000 a year in supplies. In all likelihood, however, I will[3] need considerably more than that.

For the past five years I have operated a general office supply[4] store in Idaho. When I move to Iowa, my two sons will continue to operate the Idaho store.[5]

Enclosed are the names and addresses of my references, which include several business executives in[6] Idaho. If you have any questions about my business experience, I am sure they will be glad to[7] answer them.

I look forward to meeting you, Mr. Williams. Sincerely yours, [153]

680 Dear Mrs. Ryan: Thank you for applying for credit with the Iowa Wholesale Company; your account is[1] now open. You may begin charging items at any time you wish, Mrs. Ryan.

Des Moines' business community[2] welcomes your new office supply store to our area. We are happy that you will be making our city[3] your home in the future.

Your line of credit will be $5,000. If you have occasion to charge more

than[4] this amount, just speak to our treasurer, Mr. Davis. He will be glad to arrange to increase your line of[5] credit on a temporary basis. Cordially yours, [110]

681 Dear Mr. Short: This letter will acknowledge your request for several copies of the public service circular,[1] *New Ideas in Business Correspondence*, by James Worth and Helen Underwood. Unfortunately, our[2] organization, the Wisconsin Publishing Company, does not distribute this circular. The Overmeyer[3] Publishing Company of St. Louis, Missouri, published this circular several months ago to promote[4] its correspondence materials. If you will correspond directly with them, I am sure they will send you all[5] the copies you want. Sincerely yours, [107]

682 Gentlemen: Thank you very much for responding so quickly to my request for several copies of the[1] public service circular. You are right, of course. The circular was published by the Overmeyer Publishing[2] Company of St. Louis. I have written to them, and one of their correspondents is sending me a sufficient[3] number of copies for my purposes.

I understand that your organization does occasionally[4] publish public service bulletins. I would like to have a current, up-to-date list of your circulars in print if[5] one is available. Thank you for your help. Sincerely yours, [111]

683 Dear Ms. Brice: Enclosed is my check for $100 in payment of my October bill. The check, however,[1] does not cover the entire amount billed me.

On the statement I have been charged for four purchases which I did not[2] make. They are listed as having been made on September 20, 22, 27, and 29. As[3] I was away from the city on a ten-day business trip to South Dakota at that time, I could not possibly[4] have purchased anything from your company on those dates.

Please check into the matter and deduct[5] $85, the amount of the erroneous charges, from my account. Yours very truly, [116]

684 Dear Mr. Gates: I am returning to you today the film on data processing that you sent us on approval.[1] I have viewed the film and found it to be excellent.

However, it is far too advanced for my classes. What[2] I would like is a film that would be helpful to students who know absolutely nothing about data processing[3] and the operation of computers.

If you have a film of this type, please send it to me on approval.[4] Sincerely yours, [83]

685 Dear Miss Morris: Thank you for your check for $100 to apply to your recent bill with the South[1] Carolina Wholesale Company. We appreciate your business and your prompt payment, Miss Morris.

I am sorry that[2] your records do not show the total charges of $85 made on four occasions in September. If[3] you will check with your business partner, I am sure that the problem can be solved. Our records *show** that Mr. Chase[4] purchased supplies from us on the four occasions you mention. Evidently there was a slight accounting problem in[5] your office.

Consequently, we are adding the $85 to your November bill if this is[6] satisfactory with you. If you have any questions, we will be glad to talk with you.

We are very *happy†* to serve[7] you and look forward to many years of mutually beneficial business transactions. Sincerely yours, [159]
Also correct:
*reveal, indicate
†glad

LESSON 78

689 Dear Mr. Carson: If you are still using office machines which are totally out of date while your competitors[1] are using modern, efficient computers, you are probably losing money. A business which does not keep[2] up with the competition soon begins to fall behind in profits. As I am sure you will agree, no business[3] can stand this loss.

A General computer system can put your office on a par with any other in the[4] country. A General computer can handle your accounting, payroll, and personnel records with ease and[5] efficiency. What is more, it can be installed at a price that is well within your company's budget. May I have[6] the privilege of calling on you personally this week to discuss with you the installation of a[7] General computer system? A stamped, self-addressed envelope is enclosed for your convenience in replying.[8] Very sincerely yours, [164]

690 Dear Mr. Gates: Thank you for the opportunity you offered me of visiting you and discussing with you[1] the prospect of installing a National communications system in your office. It was a pleasure to² see the inside operation of such an efficiently run organization, Mr. Gates.

I am pleased to³ report that installing a National communications system in your office can be totally accomplished⁴ in only two days.

We will be able to begin work on Monday, January 15—if this is⁵ convenient. Please let us know so that we may plan our work schedule accordingly. Very truly yours,   [117]

691 Dear Mr. Keith: January 15 will be a good day for you to begin the installation of the¹ communications system in our office. We have deferred the vacations of several of our staff members² until that time. This will allow us a great deal of flexibility in office occupancy. Some of our³ people can be transferred to the empty offices while you are installing the system in their offices.

I look⁴ forward to seeing you about 9 a.m. on January 15. Very truly yours,   [97]

692 Dear Mr. Gates: Thank you very much for offering to let us use the name of your company as a reference.¹ We certainly appreciate this, and you may expect us to take advantage of your offer in dealing² with prospective customers, both locally and nationally.

Since you offered to let us use your name in our³ advertising, it occurred to us that you might also let us use some photographs of your offices. We, of⁴ course, would pay you our regular fee for the privilege of using these photographs. Cordially yours,   [98]

693 Dear Mr. Tate: For several

years I have been considering replacing the standard filing cabinets in¹ my office, and I would like to have your opinion on the best type of files to install.

My present filing² system, which has been in use for about ten years, has six 4-drawer filing cabinets that accommodate³ letter-size papers. Although I follow a sound program of records retention, I find that the files are overcrowded⁴ most of the time. Yet I do not have room to add additional cabinets. Do you have any ideas which⁵ will help me? I will appreciate hearing from you. Very truly yours,   [113]

694 Dear Mr. Gray: Thank you for your letter asking for my opinion concerning a new filing system for your¹ office. I *believe** I understand your problem completely. You need more space for filing, but you do not have room² for more cabinets.

Fortunately, we have just the right answer for you here at the General Office Supply³ Company. I recommend that you install our six-tier vertical filing shelves, the type preferred by many⁴ executives today.

The shelves will provide much more storage space for your papers while taking less room than your present⁵ filing cabinets.

Enclosed is a circular illustrating the various *types†* of General shelf files. When⁶ you have had an opportunity to study it, I hope you will get in touch with me. I will be glad to have⁷ a representative come to your office to discuss our system with you. Sincerely yours,   [157]

Also correct:
*think
†kinds, styles

LESSON 79

698 Dear Mr. Smith: Will you please send us the following office supplies by express:

1. A ream of 50-pound bond¹ typewriter paper.
2. A carton of No. 24 general staples.
3. A box of 50 carbon² ribbons for electric typewriters.
4. A box of lightweight carbon paper.

Send the office supplies to³ 130 Park Avenue in St. Louis, Missouri; mail the bill to my Columbia address.

We are just opening⁴ a new office in St. Louis, and we need the supplies immediately. Under the circumstances I⁵ would appreciate your giving the order top priority. Very truly yours, [115]

699 Dear Mr. Madison: Thank you very much for your recent order for office supplies. As you know, this is your¹ first order for our merchandise; consequently, we are doubly pleased to receive it. We will send the supplies just² as soon as we complete a quick, routine credit check on your company's credit.

Will you please fill out and return³ the enclosed credit application form. When we receive it, we will complete our work expeditiously, and you⁴ will have the office supplies shortly thereafter. Sincerely yours,

PS. Let me congratulate you, Mr.⁵ Madison, on the opening of your new office and wish you the best of success. We hope that we will be⁶ doing business together for many years to come. [129]

700 Dear Mrs. Ford: Enclosed is my completed application form for credit with your organization. I have¹ also attached a statement giving you authority to check my financial records with the banks in which I² have accounts. I am sure you will find all my references to be quite satisfactory.

Please expedite your³ credit check so that we may receive these much-needed office supplies as quickly as possible. Thank you, Mrs.⁴ Ford, for your cooperation. It is very much appreciated. Sincerely yours, [96]

701 Dear Mr. Madison: We are happy to welcome you to our family of credit customers, which presently¹ numbers more than 5,000. We received your completed credit application form today, and we² made the necessary routine credit inquiries by telephone. Each of your references stated you have³ always handled your business with sincerity, integrity, and efficiency. The office supplies you⁴ ordered will leave our shipping room on Monday, August 15; you should have them by the end of the week.

We are sending⁵ you separately a current catalog which we hope you will use the next time you need office supplies. We know⁶ you will find our line of supplies to be of top quality and our service prompt and efficient. We look forward⁷ to serving your office needs for many years to come. Very truly yours, [153]

702 Dear Mr. Samuels: I have just had the pleasure of reading your article on the part computers play in¹ business that appeared in the June issue of *Today's Business*. As a result, I now have a better under-standing[2] of computers and data processing and their place in business.

I want to congratulate you on your[3] lucid, interesting style of writing. I hope you will write more articles for *Today's Business*. Sincerely yours, [79]

703 Dear Mrs. Wilson: Thank you for your recent order for office supplies. We *put** the first part of the shipment in[1] the mail today. The bond paper, pencils, and the electric typewriter ribbons are on their way to you now.

I[2] am sorry that we cannot at this time deliver the pens embossed with your company name. Unfortunately,[3] we are not equipped to do this type of work here in the shop. We deal with the White Manufacturing Company,[4] a supplier in South Dakota. However, they have *assured†* us they will give your order top priority.[5] If all goes well, you should have the pens in two weeks. Very truly yours, [113]
Also correct:
*placed
†told

LESSON 80

706 Gentlemen: I am considering remodeling my suite of offices in the White Building on State Street in[1] Wheeling, West Virginia. I would appreciate it if you would have one of your company's representatives[2] come to see me about doing this work.

The offices are very small, and the furnishings are quite old. The[3] storage space is inadequate, and the filing cabinets are very old-fashioned.

I believe it would be wise to[4] redesign the entire suite of offices and install the latest, most up-to-date furnishings and equipment.[5] Please write me or call me at 555-1161 to arrange an appointment. Sincerely yours, [118]

707 Dear Mr. Wilson: Thank you for your letter of Saturday, September 2. We are, of course, quite interested[1] in helping you to redesign your suite of offices in the White Building in Wheeling. As you are probably[2] aware, just last year we remodeled the national offices of the General Sweet Shops which are also[3] located in the White Building.

If it is convenient, I will come to your office on Friday, September 22,[4] at ten in the morning. I will bring along a complete set of catalogs and sample materials for[5] you to see.

Please let me know if the date and time are satisfactory. Very truly yours, [117]

708 Dear Miss Williams: It was a pleasure meeting you last week to discuss the remodeling of my offices. The[1] catalogs you left with me have been very helpful, and I have chosen a number of items which I feel will[2] make the offices more attractive as well as more functional.

When you have had an opportunity to[3] calculate the cost of doing the entire job, please forward the estimate to me. Cordially yours, [77]

709 Dear Mr. Wilson: Here are all the figures you asked me to supply. I will send you a complete breakdown of all[1] costs next week. The cost of the entire job will be $40,000, which includes installing modular walls,[2] laying new carpeting, and providing new office furniture and draperies.

It will not include, of course,[3] any office machinery you wish to replace. After you have had a chance to look over the detailed list of[4] costs, please let me know whether you want us to proceed with the work. I will be awaiting your call. Sincerely, [98]

710 Dear Mr. Sherry: Making multiple copies is one of the few processes in your office that have[1] actually come down in price over the last three or four years.

However, salaries have gone up. Consequently, the[2] cost of making a copy, in terms of employee time, has risen. The only way to bring this cost down is to[3] speed up things. That is the idea behind the Johnson 265 copier. We made it the world's fastest[4] copier.

Furthermore, the Johnson 265 will not cause problems that many other copiers do because it[5] has fewer working parts. It gives you clean, sharp copies every time.

For more information, call one of our[6] 100 offices in the United States. You will find a list of them in the enclosed booklet. Very truly[7] yours, [141]

711 Dear Mr. Smith: Does the report you dictate at 1 p.m. get typed at 2, printed at 3, and collated from[1] 4 to 7? The chances are it does. Furthermore, you probably have to pay some employees time and a half[2] for several hours.

A single report shouldn't cause any problem. It wouldn't if you had a Thomas collator.[3] One of your clerks can set up a Thomas collator in a few minutes, and 20 minutes later the work[4] is done.

Would you like more information about the Thomas collator? If you would, call us at[5] 116-1181. Sincerely yours, [105]

712 *You and Your Future*
It is always a delight to meet someone who says, "I love my work. I would not want to do anything else."

Since[1] those of us who work spend a great part of our waking hours either on the job, getting ready for the job, or[2] traveling to and from the job, it is important to try to find work that will be of interest to us.

What have[3] you done so far about your future? Do you know what you would like to do after you leave school? Have you had a[4] temporary summer or after-school job? If so, did any of those for whom you worked ask you to come back another[5] year? Were you on time for your work? Do you think you were reliable? Could you use the names of those for whom you[6] worked as references?

One high school graduate was speaking to the seniors at the school from which she was[7] graduated. She told the group that she had been surprised that the executive who hired her liked the fact that she had been[8] baby-sitting for the same family for four years. The executive said, "Our children are very important[9] to us, and if the family had you with their children for four years, they certainly must have trusted you." The[10] graduate mentioned to the seniors that the employer had checked with the parents because she had used their names as[11] references. She further told the group how important it was to ask permission before using anyone's name[12] as a reference.

When the time comes for the actual job hunting, you will never have a more important task[13] than selling yourself. In the meantime, ask yourself these questions:

1. Do I follow instructions?

2. Am I so conscientious[14] that I will stick to a job until it is not only done, but done well?

3. Are my typing and[15] shorthand skills good?

4. Am I careful to proofread the assignments I turn in so there are no spelling, punctuation,[16] or English errors?

5. Am I truly proud of the work I turn in?

6. Am I careful about my personal[17] appearance?

7. Can I take criticism?

8. Is my attendance record good?

9. Am I on time?

10. If[18] I were an employer, would I hire *me*?

If you can answer yes to eight or more of these questions, your future looks[19] bright! If you can answer five to seven with a yes, you are on the right road, but you need to make some changes. If[20] you answer yes to fewer than five, make major changes for your own sake.   [413]

APPENDIX

RECALL DRILLS

Joined Word Endings

1   Treatment, alignment, supplement, amusement, compliment, experiment.

2   Nation, termination, station, operation, inflation, relation, caution, portion, section, promotion.

3   Credential, confidential, essential, commercial, socially.

4   Greatly, namely, nicely, mainly, nearly, highly, only, properly, surely, mostly.

5   Readily, speedily, easily, hastily, necessarily, family.

6   Careful, thoughtful, delightful, mindful, usefulness, awful, helpful, powerful, respectful, faithful.

7   Dependable, reliable, profitable, table, troubled.

8   Gather, gathered, together, rather, either, leather, bother, bothered, neither, mother.

9   Actual, actually, gradual, schedule, annual, equally.

10   Furniture, picture, nature, stature, captured, miniature, failure, natural, feature.

11   Yourself, myself, itself, himself, herself, themselves, ourselves, yourselves.

12   Port, sport, import, report, deportment.

13   Contain, retain, certain, container, contained.

14   Efficient, sufficient, deficient, efficiency, deficiency, proficiency.

Disjoined Word Endings

15   Childhood, motherhood, neighborhood, brotherhood.

16   Forward, backward, onward, afterward, rewarded.

17 Relationship, steamship, authorship, professorship, championship.
18 Radical, technical, political, article, chemically, periodically, logically, practically.
19 Congratulate, regulate, stipulates, tabulated, congratulation, regulation, regulations, stipulations.
20 Willingly, exceedingly, knowingly, surprisingly, grudgingly.
21 Readings, mornings, sidings, dressings, savings, drawings, sayings, blessings, feelings, servings.
22 Program, telegram, telegrams, diagrams.
23 Notification, modification, specifications, classifications, ratification.
24 Personality, ability, reliability, facilities, utility, generalities, locality.
25 Faculty, penalty, casualty, loyalty.
26 Authority, sincerity, majority, minority, clarity, sorority, charity, seniority.

Joined Word Beginnings
27 Permit, perform, perfect, pertain, persist, purchase, pursue, pursued, purple, purse.
28 Employ, empower, embarrass, embody, empire, emphatic, embrace, emphasis, emphasize.
29 Impress, impression, imply, impossible, impair, impel, imbue, impact, imperfect.
30 Increase, intend, income, inform, inconsistent, indeed, inference, inferior, insane, inscribe.
31 Enlarge, enforce, enlist, encourage, enjoy, enrich, encounter, encircle, enrage.
32 Unkind, unwritten, unwilling, unsuccessful, undo, unpleasant, untie, unpopular.
33 Refer, resign, receive, reform, reorganize.
34 Beneath, believe, belong, before, became.
35 Delay, deliver, deserve, diligent.
36 Dismiss, disappoint, discover, discuss, despite.
37 Mistake, misquote, misspell, misstate, misunderstand, misapplied, mistrust.
38 Explain, excite, extend, excuse, express, exit.
39 Comprise, comfort, comply, completed, compete.
40 Condition, consult, continue, confident, convey, confess.
41 Submit, substantiate, subdivide, sublease, suburban.
42 Almost, also, already, although, alteration.
43 Forget, forceful, performed, forecast, foreman.
44 Furnish, furnished, furnishings, furniture, furnace, further, furtive.
45 Turn, turned, term, attorney, determine, eastern.
46 Ultimate, ulterior, adult, culture, result.

Disjoined Word Beginnings
47 Interested, internal, interview, intercept, introduce, entrance, entrances, introduction, enterprise, entertain, entered.
48 Electricity, electrician, electrical, electric wire, electric fan, electric light, electric motor, electrode.
49 Supervise, supervision, supervisor, superhuman, superb, superior.
50 Circumstance, circumstances, circumstantial, circumvent, circumspect.
51 Selfish, self-made, self-defense, self-respect, self-conscious, self-assured.

52 Transit, transfer, transact, transplant, translation.

53 Understand, undertake, undergo, underpaid, undermine, understate, underline, underscore, understood, undercover.

54 Overcome, overdue, overhead, overture, overpay, oversee, overdraw, overgrow, overlook, overnight, oversight.

Key to Chart on Page 448

Brief Forms of Gregg Shorthand in Alphabetical Order

1 A-an, about, acknowledge, advantage, advertise, after, am.

2 And, any, are-our-hour, be-by, business, but, can.

3 Character, characters, circular, company, correspond-correspondence, corresponded, could.

4 Difficult, doctor, enclose, envelope, every-ever, executive, experience.

5 For, from, general, gentlemen, glad, good, govern.

6 Government, have, I, idea, immediate, important-importance, innot.

7 Is-his, it-at, manufacture, morning, Mr., Mrs., Ms.

8 Never, newspaper, next, object, objected, of, one (won).

9 Opinion, opportunity, order, ordinary, organize, out, over.

10 Part, particular, present, probable, progress, public, publish-publication.

11 Quantity, question, recognize, regard, regular, request, responsible.

12 Satisfy-satisfactory, send, several, short, should, soon, speak.

13 State, street, subject, success, suggest, than, thank.

14 That, the, them, there (their), they, thing-think, this.

15 Throughout, time, under, usual, value, very, was.

16 Were, what, when, where, which, will-well, wish.

17 With, work, world, worth, would, yesterday, you-your.